WAITING FOR NERDROTIC

From Prison to YouTube

By Gary Buechler

ADVANCE PRAISE FOR
WAITING FOR NERDROTIC

"*Waiting for Nerdrotic* is a true American success story of a phoenix that rose from the ashes."

—Graham Nolan, 2014 Inkpot Award winner
and artist for DC Comics

"Gary Buechler's meteoric rise in *Waiting for Nerdrotic* is both inspiring and something to marvel at. He so eloquently speaks on behalf of the *fans*, and that's why so many people gravitate towards him."

—Eric July, comic book writer, YouTuber
and lead vocalist of BackWordz

"*Waiting for Nerdrotic* is an inspirational and relatable life story that should inspire you to get off your ass and do your own thing."

—Chris Gore, head writer and founder of *Film Threat*,
former producer, writer and host of *Attack of the Show*

PRAISE FOR GARY BUECHLER

"In a world overrun by shills and so-called entertainment 'journalists,' Gary Buechler is a beacon of truth in a land of cowards. If you want to know what the Hollywood trade publications will be writing about in a few years, his Nerdrotic YouTube channel—where he has become a veritable Nerdstradamus predicting entertainment trends well before they become blatantly obvious to everyone—is a must-watch. More than a passionate fan, his historical knowledge of comics, TV and movies is beyond encyclopedic. He consistently speaks aloud the things that everyone can clearly see, but are frozen in fear to speak aloud. Buechler's bravery is to be admired."

—Chris Gore, head writer and founder of *Film Threat*, former producer, writer and host of *Attack of the Show*

"Gary is one of the most genuine and interesting guys I've met—someone who has experienced the lowest of lows, turned his whole life around and is now enjoying the success he very much deserves."

—The Critical Drinker, entertainment YouTuber

ISBN: 978-1-964377-25-4 (ebook)

ISBN: 978-1-964377-21-6 (paperback)

ISBN: 978-1-964377-26-1 (hardcover)

DEDICATION

To my parents, Arvin and Linda.

This book is dedicated to my father, whose spirit lives on
in every challenge I face and every triumph I achieve.
If my father could witness my journey,
I know he would still be completely perplexed by it.
And to my mother who always asks me about my "radio show"
—my radio show is doing fine.

Thank you for everything.

TABLE OF CONTENTS

GREETINGS, AND WELCOME TO WAITING FOR NERDROTIC.

EVERYONE HAS A STORY. THIS IS MINE.

IT'S CALLED THAT BECAUSE THAT'S THE MESSAGE THAT SHOWS UP ON YOUTUBE LIVESTREAMS WHEN I'M A BIT LATE SHOWING UP.

WHICH, IF I'M HONEST... HAPPENS A LOT.

1986

THIS STORY MIGHT BE JUST THE THING FOR YOU. OR IT MIGHT NOT. SEE, IT ALL DEPENDS...

...ON HOW YOU FEEL ABOUT RECOVERY AND SOBRIETY.

1992

IT'S A GOOD BET THAT IF YOU'RE READING THIS, SOMEONE IN YOUR WORLD HAS BEEN AFFECTED BY ADDICTION OR ALCOHOLISM.

BUT IF YOU THINK RECOVERY IS A CLICHE THAT PEOPLE TALK ABOUT TOO DAMN MUCH WHEN THEY'RE SHARING THEIR LIFE STORY...

2009

...THIS BOOK MIGHT NOT BE FOR YOU.

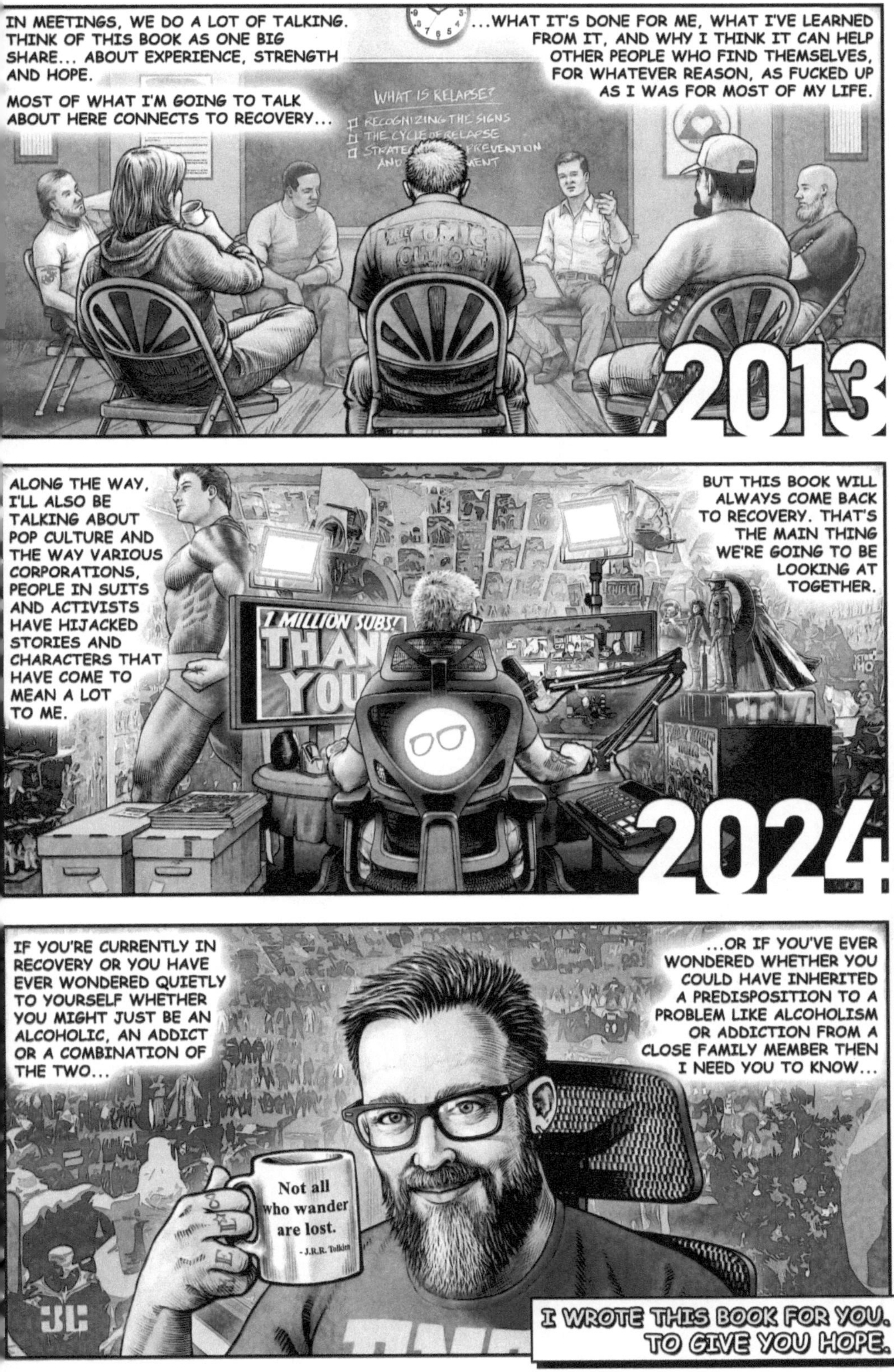

IN MEETINGS, WE DO A LOT OF TALKING. THINK OF THIS BOOK AS ONE BIG SHARE... ABOUT EXPERIENCE, STRENGTH AND HOPE.

MOST OF WHAT I'M GOING TO TALK ABOUT HERE CONNECTS TO RECOVERY...

...WHAT IT'S DONE FOR ME, WHAT I'VE LEARNED FROM IT, AND WHY I THINK IT CAN HELP OTHER PEOPLE WHO FIND THEMSELVES, FOR WHATEVER REASON, AS FUCKED UP AS I WAS FOR MOST OF MY LIFE.

WHAT IS RELAPSE?
☐ RECOGNIZING THE SIGNS
☐ THE CYCLE OF RELAPSE
☐ STRATEG... ...PREVENTION AND ...MENT

2013

ALONG THE WAY, I'LL ALSO BE TALKING ABOUT POP CULTURE AND THE WAY VARIOUS CORPORATIONS, PEOPLE IN SUITS AND ACTIVISTS HAVE HIJACKED STORIES AND CHARACTERS THAT HAVE COME TO MEAN A LOT TO ME.

BUT THIS BOOK WILL ALWAYS COME BACK TO RECOVERY. THAT'S THE MAIN THING WE'RE GOING TO BE LOOKING AT TOGETHER.

1 MILLION SUBS!
THANK YOU

2024

IF YOU'RE CURRENTLY IN RECOVERY OR YOU HAVE EVER WONDERED QUIETLY TO YOURSELF WHETHER YOU MIGHT JUST BE AN ALCOHOLIC, AN ADDICT OR A COMBINATION OF THE TWO...

...OR IF YOU'VE EVER WONDERED WHETHER YOU COULD HAVE INHERITED A PREDISPOSITION TO A PROBLEM LIKE ALCOHOLISM OR ADDICTION FROM A CLOSE FAMILY MEMBER THEN I NEED YOU TO KNOW...

Not all who wander are lost.
- J.R.R. Tolkien

I WROTE THIS BOOK FOR YOU. TO GIVE YOU HOPE.

PROLOGUE: BEFORE WE JUMP IN...

Some people say everyone has a life story that's worth writing about. I'm really hoping that's true.

I'm assuming that, if you're reading this, you've seen my YouTube channel. That's generally how most people know me: from YouTube. So before I start telling you about what growing up was like for me, let me tell you this: Ever since I started work on this book, I've had this feeling that I would need to begin it by sharing the reason I got into YouTube in the first place...and that I should follow that up with the biggest lesson I've learned from being on YouTube. So that's what I'm going to do.

Once we've covered those two things, we can start working our way through the whole messy timeline I've traced out over the past five decades. That timeline tells a story about finding the road to recovery and staying on that road. But the reason I became a YouTuber, and the lesson I learned from doing that as my day job, connects to everything that I have to tell you about that story. Everything I've learned from the long series of epic, fucked-up choices I've made, and everything I have to share about how I started making better choices.

The *reason* I got into *YouTube*...and the single biggest *lesson* I learned from being a YouTuber...are the two big takeaways from this book.

So let's start with those two things.

The Reason I Got Into YouTube

Long before I made a single YouTube video, I was a traumatized and delinquent kid and a convicted felon who had already been in and out of the penal system. I'd gotten sober, started working as a driver delivering auto parts and got married and divorced before I became the Nerdrotic most people know today.

In some of my earliest memories, it was comic books, superheroes and all things pop culture that helped me survive—and the second chapter of my life after getting sober (the first time) began with owning and operating a comic book store in San Francisco…until I damn near killed myself and damn near lost my family.

My addiction got so out of control that my wife, Melissa, kicked me out of our house. After I got cleaned up (the second time) and she decided I was clean and sober enough to be let back into the house, we realized we were facing a problem: We were not only broken. We were also *broke*.

Only an intervention from the people I loved *kept* me from dying, losing my family or hitting the addiction jackpot of doing both those things at the exact same time. The intervention was what finally persuaded me to take getting clean seriously—to see my drug addiction as the life-and-death issue it had become.

As I got sober, it occurred to me that this was not my first trip down this self-and-family-destructive path.[1] I remember thinking: *Statistically speaking, I probably shouldn't even be alive.* For some reason, though, I was. Once upon a time, I had been the owner and operator of a successful business—but that income source was gone now.

Maybe, I thought, *there's a reason behind all this.* And I started to get curious about what that reason might be. *Hmm…maybe my gargantuan cocaine habit had something to do with that?*

To get more money flowing into the household and to supplement Melissa's income, I interviewed for a job that would take me back to a better salary and an old profession: my skilled trade, auto parts. I wasn't crazy about this career direction, but I didn't see a lot of other options. We needed money.

Maybe my gargantuan cocaine habit had something to do with that, too.
So, I got a job at Tesla.

Going back to auto parts was really tough for me. The benefits were good and the pay was all right (but not great), but the job was deadly dull. It certainly didn't inspire me. You have to understand that running the comic book store—setting up the environment, finding ways to promote it, coming up with interesting new questions to ask customers—all of that had been a major creative outlet for me. Now, my typical working day had zero creativity.

There were all these Tesla corporate rules I had to follow, some of which didn't make a lot of sense (and as you'll see in the later chapters, following rules really isn't my strong suit).

Bottom line: I wasn't happy with my work. Not being happy was a problem I had, a few months earlier, been "solving" with cocaine (notice the quotation marks). So, I knew I had to come up with a different solution if I was going to make recovery work.

One of the rules at Tesla was that you weren't supposed to watch videos or play games—or have personal conversations, for that matter—on your cell phone. But there I was, bored out of my mind nine hours a day, doing a job I knew I could do with total safety and total efficiency in my sleep… and so I broke the rules. I started watching YouTube videos on the sly.

Now, remember: This was at a time in my life when it was really essential to my recovery that I find a way to feel good enough to get through the day. And surprise, surprise—secretly watching YouTube made getting through the day *easier!* It made *sobriety* easier! There was something about watching certain videos, the ones that connected to what I now call **nerd culture**, that made me feel better.

In particular, there were three creators that helped get me through: Geeks & Gamers (specifically Jeremy), World Class Bullshitters and Yellowflash. **Watching their YouTube videos made me feel a little less alone.**

YouTube began providing the same kind of payoff that listening to hours and hours of talk radio gave me back when I was driving around delivering auto parts. Like talk radio, YouTube, was company. It was engagement.

It was connection. It was a "sobriety buddy." And I needed all three of those things.

Watching videos on topics I was passionate about made me feel a little more connected in what would have otherwise been a very lonely time. YouTube made me feel like I belonged, like I could and would get through the day. Those feelings were the reason *why* I eventually started thinking about starting my own channel on the platform.

Experiencing that feeling of connection and of getting through the day intact made me curious about what was possible. Maybe other people needed that same sense of belonging I needed. Maybe *I* could help people feel connected, when they really needed connection. After trying and failing to run a comic shop, maybe that was a way I could be *good* at something again. After all, connecting with customers had made them feel like *they* belonged. What if I could do that on a much *bigger* scale by talking about nerd culture?

Nerd Culture: The ideas, customs and social behaviors of people who are unashamed about expressing their opinions and enthusiasm about media content that matters to them on a personal level.

Maybe *that* was why I had gone through all the crazy shit I had gone through: so I could engage with people who needed contact as badly as I did. Maybe I could make them feel less lonely, less on their own, less isolated. Maybe talking about pop culture, which I loved, could become my **fixed point of nerddom**. It was something that we all had in common. My passion for *that* topic was what could make me more creative and more connected.

I started my YouTube channel to help myself by helping other people. I wanted to help working people feel connected to each other and connected to culture again so we would all feel less alone.

Fast forward a decade or so, and I cannot count the number of people who have written to me, messaged me or walked up to me unannounced and told me that the Nerdrotic channel has helped them get through hard times: **recovery, divorce, unemployment, the passing of a loved one, the global pandemic or just the day-in, day-out of a job that makes their head hurt.**

So that's why I started the YouTube channel. For them, and for me. It's why I'm *still* doing it, and it's why I'm writing this book.

The Big Lesson I've Learned from Launching a YouTube Channel

There's a myth out there that believing in yourself is the key to success. In my experience, that's bullshit.

You can believe in yourself all day long and not get anywhere. It's more about believing in something you love, something that brings you joy.

If I hadn't been talking about something I loved, the channel would not have connected with me or with anyone else. It wouldn't have been authentic.

Now that we've looked at the big *reason* and the big *lesson*, we can move on to the official timeline. The first entry there is my birthday, August 19, 1969—which happens to be the day after Long John Silver's, the big seafood restaurant chain, opened its very first store. Interesting coincidence: At one point in my life, I was living under a bush in front of a Long John Silver's...

...but I'm getting ahead of myself.

Anyway—time for Part One.

PART ONE: BREAKING BAD

In Part One, I have a fucked-up childhood, stop going to school and get into trouble with the law. My life pretty much sucks. The only escape from the trauma and hard times is nerddom. I dive head-first into pop culture, inhaling Star Wars, Tolkien and Marvel the way Keith Richards and Mick Jagger inhaled the blues.

1. HARBINGER OF HATE

As near as I can make out, I was born addicted.

I say this based on conversations I had with my birth mother as an adult, once I connected with her. She was 16 years old when she had me in August 1969, and she had been doing a lot of different drugs while she was pregnant with me. I don't call the guy who got her pregnant my father, because he wasn't. I never met him. Let's just call him the sperm donor.

From what I've been able to piece together, he was in his early 20s and extremely religious. My birth mom told me he was a very active member of the Seventh-day Adventist Church. Religion or no religion though, he took off on her and was nowhere to be found when she gave birth at a place called Booth Memorial Hospital in San Diego, which is now not a hospital at all, but a freeway on-ramp.

Even when it was a hospital, it wasn't much of a hospital. It was run by The Salvation Army exclusively as a place where unwed mothers could go to give birth. So yes, there were doctors on hand, but no, it wasn't what you think of when you hear the word hospital. It was the lowest tier of the 1969 healthcare system.

So, basically, I was born addicted—at the Salvation Army.

A couple short months after I was born, I was adopted by Arvin Buechler, a hard-working navy veteran who had made it through a tough childhood in South Dakota and his devoted wife Linda—but let me hit pause here for a moment.

I know it's very common for people who write books like this to look for reasons to throw their parents under the bus, but that's not something that I'm going to do here—and not just because my dad is no longer with us and my mom is frail. It's because I know for a fact these were good-hearted people with great intentions and classically-60's, middle-American values who were having trouble conceiving a child. They heard about the opportunity to adopt one, and they stepped up and made a lifelong commitment to be the best parents they possibly could. They did everything in their power to fulfill that commitment, and they did the best job possible that they or anyone else could've done. My adopted parents got stuck with the job of raising me, and I was *not* an easy kid to raise. That's the truth, and I won't be implying anything else about them anywhere in this book.

It's also true, though, that they had no idea what they were walking into (though, for that matter, neither did I).

Sometimes people ask me how I can be so certain that I've always been an addict even though I'm not quite sure which specific drugs my birth mother was on. This is based on my own personal instincts, and also on something I learned about addict behavior as an adult.

When I was a kid, I obviously didn't have drugs around, but I was obsessive in a way that addicts are obsessive. From the very earliest days, I had little or no impulse control. An early memory I have is of coming home with a bag full of Halloween candy and being told not to eat at all in one night…and eating it all in one sitting anyway.

I also had an obsession with collecting stuff that has persisted to this day. It's how I was born: obsessive and with no discipline at all. Even if I had made it through second grade without incident, my adoptive parents would have still gotten much, much more than they bargained for after signing the papers. And as you've probably already guessed, I *didn't* make it through second grade without incident.

This next part is heavy: When I was six years old, my teacher molested me multiple times, and his routine was to do it while the rest of the class was watching a movie. My best estimate is that this man sexually assaulted me about four or five times, but of course, I was very young. It's possible it happened slightly less or slightly more—and though I'm comfortable talking about it now, I sure as hell wasn't comfortable with it when it was happening to me.

What I do know for sure is that it happened on more than one occasion and that he threatened to kill me if I told anyone. Whether he meant it or just said it to scare, I don't even fucking know, but it doesn't matter. He kept threatening me, it kept happening and I didn't tell *anyone*.

One of the times this happened, I bolted, leaving the school grounds and heading for home. Try to imagine what has to happen for a second grader to decide it's time to just walk away and disappear from school. There was no bus to ride in the middle of the school day and my house was about six miles away, but I *knew* I needed to go home—and I also knew I couldn't tell anyone exactly *why* I had to leave. I didn't have the vocabulary to process what I was going through, even if I had wanted to tell someone about it. I was just determined to get out of there to a safe place.

I walked *five miles* before the bus driver who usually drove me home saw me walking and picked me up, all at the age of six. I walked right the fuck out of school and got in big trouble for it, too.

That five-mile walk was one of the reasons I flunked second grade. My parents thought I'd just lost it and had some kind of temper tantrum. The teachers decided this episode was evidence I was a problem child. What kind of six-year-old just walks out of class? One who's trouble, that's who.

Looking back now, I feel sure in my bones that the people who held positions of authority in the school knew exactly what was going on. They fucking knew this man was a predator, and they kept him on for another year. I wasn't in the same class the next year, but I still had to act as though nothing had happened. The teachers' union protected abusive teachers back then, and they still protect plenty of teachers now who shouldn't be teaching. I think my issues with unions go back to this experience.

After that first experience, school became a daily nightmare for me, and I've blocked a lot of the memories of it. I don't remember much else about the aftermath of those attacks, beyond being terrified every time I set foot on school grounds. My academic performance cratered, and I had to repeat second grade. More important than any of the academic stuff, though, was the reprogramming going on in my head because of that repeated abuse. A child's brain does what it needs to do after trauma, after all; it's a matter of survival.

In my case, that rewiring took the form of a deep and abiding mistrust of—no, let's be real about it, an abiding *hatred* of—authority. There was the occasional teachers I could find a way to get along with, but I knew for a *fact* that school was a fucked-up, scary place to be. I just did not trust *any* adults other than my mom and my dad, and I wasn't inclined to give them the benefit of the doubt, either.

If you were an adult telling me what to do, my attitude towards you from about age six onwards was pretty consistently as follows: *Fuck you. Fuck all of this.*

Sometime in 1975, the same year I was in second grade, another life-changing event happened. My memory is a little scrambled, so I'm not sure if it was before or after I was abused (though if I had to bet on it, I think it was after). What matters is that I walked into a 7-11 on Rancho Santa Fe Road in San Diego, and saw *Marvel Team-Up #42* featuring Spider-Man and The Vision.

As I stared at that cover of that comic book, I realized that nothing was ever going to be the same. I had to have it—my life somehow wouldn't be complete unless I *did* have it. It was one of the most pivotal moments of my life.[2]

I've asked myself many times over the years *why* seeing that particular comic book was such an important moment for me. Maybe there was something stunning and unexpected about the drawn image of Spider-Man that stopped me cold?

At that time, my experience of superheroes came from two main sources: George Reeves's TV *Superman* (from reruns of 1950s episodes) and Adam West's TV *Batman* (from reruns of 1960s episodes). I liked those shows, but this was something new. Something different. Something more inspiring and mysterious and exciting. Something I had to find out about. That much was non-negotiable. Even as a six-year old, maybe I could sense that.

Why was it non-negotiable? Who knows. Maybe it was the fact that Spider-Man was (unlike those other two guys I had seen on TV) *totally covered* by his costume, and particularly by his mask. This wasn't some guy whose secret identity depended on glasses or a cowl that only covered the top half of his face. This guy had gone all the way. He had completely submerged himself in the superhero role he had taken on.

And what a costume it was. That red, that deep blue, those web patterns, those odd white shapes that hid the eyes…I was hooked. Something about a mask that entirely covered the face spoke to me at a very deep level. Maybe I saw the possibility that I could reinvent myself like Spider-Man had, or maybe the costume just reminded me of the Mexican wrestlers I had seen on TV, who were cool, too.

Or maybe that weird dark villain on horseback that Spider-Man and the Vision were taking on reminded me of some authority figure. Someone I didn't like at all.

I don't remember how it happened, but I know I left that store with that comic book in my hand. I like to think my mother bought it for me. The minute I opened it up and started reading it, I knew I was home.

When third grade rolled around, I started attending a new school that opened closer to my house. The good thing about it was I no longer had to worry about crossing paths with the teacher who abused me. The bad part was I was still processing deep trauma, and now, I would have to do it in a new environment without any of my friends around.

At least I still had Spider-Man.

2. ESCAPE

I was part of a pretty normal suburban family, but I never felt like I fit in. Comic books didn't make me fit in any better, but they did bring me a lot of joy.

Another thing that brought me joy was *The Lord of the Rings*. No, I didn't read the J.R.R. Tolkien saga at the age of seven (that would come much later), but I *do* remember being totally transfixed by the Rankin/Bass animated version, which was weird and cool and impossible to ignore. Frodo had some crazy, crazy shit to deal with, and watching him handle it made me feel safe. I couldn't look away.

This isn't a normal cartoon, I thought. *I hope it never ends.*

One of the great things about finding a source of entertainment that really touches you is that it provides a little relief. It can be a little escape from the harder things that are going on in your life. Good entertainment helps you *process* the hard stuff; it makes it a little bit easier to handle the feeling that you're all alone.

The next time I had a similar experience was when I was seven years old, and my mom took me to the movies to see the first *Star Wars* film. Back in 1977, it was just called *Star Wars*, and it rocked my little world watching Luke, Leia, Han and Chewie go up against Darth Vader and the Evil Empire. It was another one of those moments where I just knew, instantly, in my bones, that I was home.

Over the years, I would learn that I wasn't the only one in my family who'd been through strange and difficult shit at a very young age. My dad, for instance, had a truly brutal childhood—one that was almost as chaotic as mine. My father, Arvin Buechler,[3] was born in South Dakota, in a little town called Roscoe with a population of only about 300 people. His family was dirt poor, his mom was disabled as the result of botched surgery and his dad died when he was six.

My dad and his brother, Verlin, ended up working very long hours on a farm when they were just six or seven years old. When they were old enough, they both joined the Navy at the same time, more or less, to get out of Roscoe (from what I've managed to figure out, at least). It was how my dad ended up in San Diego, where he met my mom. Just like me, my dad had gone through a lot of shit that couldn't possibly make sense to a young kid. Growing up, we actually had a lot in common, though it wouldn't become clear to either of us for years.[4]

At that time, I didn't feel like I had very much in common with anyone—except Spider-Man, Luke Skywalker, Frodo Baggins, the Vision, the Green Lantern, the Fantastic Four, Dr. Strange, Ghost Rider…people like that. Somehow, *they* seemed to know where I was coming from, but principals and parents? Not so much.

A big part of the problem was connected to the era I grew up in. If I 'd gone through the public school system three or four decades later, I would have been diagnosed with ADHD. The teachers and administrators at a halfway-decent school would have been responsible for that diagnosis, and they would've had to make some reasonable accommodations for a kid like me. But this was the mid-70s. Instead, I was typecast as unruly and disruptive. Generally speaking, I was a "bad" kid.

My ADHD made me restless. I wasn't crazy about sitting still for long periods of time, I didn't follow along in the book as well as some of the other kids did and I lost interest very quickly and things that were, well, dull. Of course, none of that made me *bad*. Feeling helpless, let down, confused and unable to cope with the trauma of abuse didn't make me bad, either.

Being *treated* like a bad kid by teachers and administrators, on the other hand? I think that *did* turn me into a bad kid. Most teachers disciplined me and tried to make me feel like shit, and I always took that personally. I didn't forget and I held grudges. It was your basic no-win situation.

For the most part, I just did not pay much attention or care too much about anything going on in school, with the possible exceptions of sports and the occasional cool teacher. For some reason, most coaches on sports teams I signed up for quickly figured out how to interact with me. Occasionally I'd even run into a teacher who was kind and cool and didn't judge me or make me do things based on their position or authority. Who didn't punish me or humiliate me just because they could. Every once in a while, I'd run into a teacher who understood that I didn't do well in an environment where I had to agree in advance to follow a lot of rules and pretend that I was like every other kid. I *didn't* agree to that, I *didn't* feel bad when I broke the rules and I *wasn't* like other kids. I knew that, but the *teachers* who grasped it were fewer and farther in between.

Most of the time, my teachers and I were at war. They thought that unless they were imposing the structure of school on me, reciting rules and regulations and demanding that I give explanations in front of the class— or unless they were passing judgment on me when I didn't follow those rules and regulations—they weren't doing their job. I didn't care much for rules and regulations, and I didn't mind saying so. From their point of view, I was constantly disrespecting them and disrupting the class. Which, to be fair, I was. It was a cycle that didn't do anyone any good.

I had learned the hard way, very early on, that there were some really bad adults out there. My working assumption was that *most* of them were bad, and that there wasn't any point in cutting them slack, since they certainly weren't going to cut me any. Every day at school, and I do mean *every* day, I got more evidence that backed up my assumptions. There came a point when I lost all interest in the game of trying to make teachers like me when it was clear and obvious that they didn't.

School was more than just a drag. It was something I knew I had to literally, physically escape from—but I hadn't yet created a strategy or found the resources necessary to do it. Breaking out was really what I wanted, but I couldn't do it yet. Instead, I did the next best thing: I retreated into solitude, into my own little world. I did that a *whole* lot, mostly by diving deeper and deeper into television and comic books I wasn't supposed to bring to school but did. In fact, I got addicted to comic books. Truthfully, I hoarded them.

The interesting thing about my comic book fixation is that it was the first addiction I can remember worrying about *funding*—no joke. It was a serious problem for me that I didn't have the money to buy all the comics I wanted. So, I got a paper route. It might have looked from the outside that moving from unemployed to having a job was a positive shift, driven by sharpening my personal initiative, developing a better attitude toward work, contributing to society…stuff like that. What was really driving me, though, was an addiction. At nine years old, I was hooked on comics.

I basically started mainlining comic books, following a lot of stories from what we would now call the Marvel and DC Universes. But the one that had the biggest impact on me as I made my way forward was Spider-Man.

Peter Parker fascinated me. Authority figures—like his boss, J. Jonah Jameson—were always yelling at him and treating him badly. He'd suffered major losses in his life, like the loss of his parents and the death of his Uncle Ben. He had huge daily problems to deal with: He was always struggling to take care of his Aunt May, who had major medical issues, and he always faced major financial challenges. His life was a mess, but he became this whole other individual, Spider-Man, and somehow always found a way to do the right thing. In every issue, despite his hang-ups, his problems and the obstacles people threw at him, he always found a way to save the person who needed saving. He never stopped trying to figure out how to do the right thing, and eventually, he always found it.

I wouldn't have put it this way back then, but it's obvious to me now as I look back: Peter Parker gave me hope. That was important, because hope was something I didn't have a whole lot of on any given school day. For the most part, it all seemed pretty fucking pointless to me.

3. THIS ISN'T HAPPENING

I started drinking and partying at the age of 12.

That's a pretty absurd sentence to write, but it's the truth, and I know I'm not the only one who started partying that early. At first, my sister, who was five years older than I was, would ask her boyfriend (who was over 18) to throw me a beer once in a while. I discovered I could get wasted on half a beer, and soon, getting wasted was what I started to look forward to.

I started looking for other older kids who would throw me a beer once in a while, and I also started smoking pot around the same age. It wasn't a regular thing, but if I happened to be hanging out with kids who were smoking it, they would give me a hit. I didn't seek it out, but I did spend a lot of time with kids who smoked, so I ended up doing my fair share of toking (even if I didn't enjoy it as much as drinking alcohol). From there, it all escalated, because that's how addiction works.

I started partying more heavily in the middle of my freshman year in high school. Right around the Christmas break, I stopped being interested in pretty much anything that didn't connect to going to parties, listening to music—Metallica was particularly important to me and the people I hung out with—and getting wasted. After that, things started to fall apart in a way that was impossible for the people around me not to notice.

I had made the football team at the beginning of the year…but then I got kicked off the team because I wasn't showing up for practices. Earlier in the year, sports had been an important part of my life. Now, I had stopped caring—about football or anything that wasn't partying, reading comic books[5] or listening to metal music. I got a lot of lectures from my dad as well as former coaches and teachers about how important it was for me to turn things around, but I tuned all of them out.

There were a couple of downsides to all of this. One major downside was that I was perpetually short on cash, and I knew I needed a plan to deal with that. Another was that my performance in school was cratering. This wasn't a problem for me personally, but my parents seemed concerned, which meant more consequences at home for me to deal with.

Another significant downside, the one that bothered me most, was this creeping feeling of dread—this strange sensation I could never seem to shake that I was doing something wrong and I would pay for it later. No problem, I thought. *Getting high makes the dread go away, at least for a little while.* So that's what I did: I got high. That was my antidote to all the depression and confusion and anxiety I was feeling. I knew the consequences would arrive at some point, but I planned to put them off for as long as I could. My strategy was to crank up Metallica, getting really fucking high and pretend that everything that was happening wasn't happening.

4. A CONVERSATION WITH A TEACHER

I have a one-liner I often use about the next fascinating period of my life that goes like this:

I'm the only person I know who got kicked out of three high schools in a row.

But even though it gets a laugh, it's not really accurate. What actually happened was that I got kicked out of *two* high schools in a row, and the third school wanted nothing to do with me. My reputation preceded me.

How had things gotten so bad? Looking back, I can see it was a series of progressively worse decisions. Part of me knew damn well that I was heading for a day of reckoning and that all my choices were bringing it closer, but it didn't matter. High school felt like a prison to me, and I needed a way to bust out of it.[6]

I always had the same gnawing feeling: *I hate this, I don't fit in here, this isn't for me.* At the same time, I was acutely aware that *I* was the one fucking things up for myself. I was heading into a storm that would only get worse, all because of my own bad choices. I knew I was putting off dealing with all my problems and that, at some point, there would be hell to pay. I was making bad decisions and I knew it—and I kept right on making them.

I had been ditching classes left and right and going to school drunk and high. I had even started stealing things to finance my comic book addiction at first, before stealing to finance...other things.[7] It wasn't that I didn't *know* these were stupid decisions; that was obvious to me, and I worried about it all the fucking time. The more bad decisions I made, the more I worried, and the more I worried, the worse I felt. I was never suicidal, but I was still incredibly down all the time—a little further down each day, it seemed.

Unless I was high, of course.

So, of course, whenever I found myself feeling worse than I had the day before—whenever I spiraled into an intense cycle of worry about what the storm would feel like when it finally hit full force—it was easy enough for me to make myself stop worrying about everything. All I had to do was party like it was 1999. That solved everything!

It probably comes as no surprise that I partied like it was 1999 too many times for a freshman in high school. I also showed up to school wasted too many times and I ditched too many classes. Finally, they suspended my ass, and from there, I went to what was known as a continuation school: Sunset High School, down the street from our house.

What was weird about this school was that it had kids who were very academically advanced and kids who were struggling academically and socially (like me). It was like they took the opposite ends of the bell curve and nobody in the middle and decided to build a school around it. The result was two sets of kids who had the fewest possible things in common with each other. It was a very polarized situation, but it didn't make me more academically inclined. Instead, I spent all of my time with the metalheads and punk rockers, making it my mission to prove to them I wasn't a poseur.

All my new friends and I would do was organize parties, go out and get into all kinds of trouble. The courses we were taking were Get Out of Your Mind Wasted and another that I loved called Skateboard Dangerously Fast Without Any Protective Equipment. I was also enrolled in Generally, Wreak Fucking Havoc. It was all self-paced instruction, and though it took some effort, I pulled it off.

At some point, someone gave me a line of speed, and just a few seconds after I snorted it, the most amazing, unexpected thing happened: everything seemed to make sense. It wasn't what I expected, but I went with it. Suddenly, life was moving forward in whatever direction I wanted, and I could do anything I needed to do. If I did a line of speed, I could even do my homework—something I usually did a pretty good job of avoiding.[8]

If I did a line of speed, I could organize my comic books. If I did a line of speed, I could clean my room. As long as I was high on speed, I decided, everything clicked and life became doable—I even started drawing a lot. All I had to do was conceal the fact that I was taking speed from my parents. And teachers. And law enforcement. And, of course, come up with the money to buy my own speed when I couldn't get it for free from other people.[9]

I had really developed a taste for crank, but I was still drinking a lot too, of course. If you're keeping score at home, by the time I was 18, I was a heavy drinker, a speed freak and a crystal meth addict. I was already a substance abuse prodigy, a renaissance addict, and all before being legally considered an adult. I was doing just about everything, and I was having a great time doing it.[10] There's a line from a Rolling Stones song that comes to mind: "I wasn't looking very good, but I was feeling great." Other days, I looked okay, but I kind of felt like shit.

Sunset was the worst possible place to send someone in my situation. I was partying more than ever, hanging with the wrong crowd, doing all kinds of drugs and drinking like crazy. I was making even more idiotic choices than I had been at my old school. One that stands out in particular was the decision to steal a car from a teacher my buddies and I didn't like.

I don't remember what our endgame was for that little stunt, but the car ended up in a ditch. Actually, I don't think we worked out an endgame. I guess we thought we were making a statement, and that was as far as we got. Don't ask me how, but *somehow*, we didn't get busted for that one—and believe it or not, my other big Sunset memory is an even more epic fuck up than that was.

***

One afternoon, I got called on the carpet for doing something that was incredibly stupid, and the teacher I didn't like made me stay after class (probably about constantly ditching classes, I thought, which I had gotten pretty good at and was actually kind of proud of). I know it wasn't about stealing that car, because I remember being paranoid that the teacher would find out about the car incident the entire time.[11]

Once his classroom was empty, the teacher got up from his desk, walked to where I was sitting and looked me dead in the eye.

"Buechler," he said finally, "I've had enough of you."

I looked right back. "Yeah?" I replied. "Is that right?"

"It absolutely is right. I've had more than my fill of you. Way more."

"You don't say."

"Yeah, I do—I do say. You are wasting my time, Buechler. You're wasting *everyone's* time here. We both know you don't belong here at Sunset. You are never going to amount to anything, ever. And as far as I'm concerned, I want you out of here."

I stood up. "Really?"

"Really," he replied.

"I've got the most amazing coincidence to share with you: I want the same goddamned thing," I said. "So here's my idea: What if you *go fuck yourself?*"

And that's when he started screaming. I'd never seen or heard a teacher actually scream like that before. His face got all red. It was really impressive.

"*Buechler!*" he screeched, loud enough for everybody in the building to hear. "You cannot talk to a teacher like that, you *useless piece of shit!*"

As we stared each other down, I thought for a couple of seconds about what the best comeback to that might be. Finally, it came to me: I punched him in the mouth. Hard.

He went down fast and didn't come back up. I figured the best choice was to leave, so at that point, I did.

It was the second school I got kicked out of, but I suppose I should have been grateful that the teacher didn't press assault charges (or grand theft auto, for that matter). But I *wasn't* grateful. As far as I was concerned, the real problem was that the teacher had been acting like an asshole.

Things started to go downhill from there. A couple of weeks passed, maybe a month, as my parents tried to get me enrolled at Carlsbad, another high school. They knew a good friend of mine who they liked went to Carlsbad, and they thought he might be a good influence on me. Maybe he would have been, but we never got the chance to find out.

The teacher I punched in the mouth had spread word to every high school principal in the district that I was bad news, which, to be fair, I was. My dad got a phone call informing him that I would not be attending Carlsbad. That phone call marked the formal end of my high school career. Like I said, my reputation preceded me.

What I remember thinking at the time was: *I am completely fucking up my life. Oh, well. Let's get high.*

5. SERIOUS SHIT

I tell everyone that Melissa and I knew each other from high school, although that's not technically accurate. We *met* in high school, but we only got to *know* each other outside of school grounds. In other words: the times when we were each *supposed* to be going to high school, but weren't.

Come to think of it, the very first time I saw her was at a movie theater. One rainy afternoon, a couple of buddies and I were ditching class to watch the film Airplane![12] There were only half a dozen people in the whole theater besides us, and two of them were kids our age: a guy and a girl. Even in the dark theater, lit only by the movie screen, I couldn't stop looking at her. There was something about her face that drew me in like a magnet.

When the movie ended, we went out into the lobby to play video games, and she and her date came out, too. I tried to play it cool and make it look like she wasn't on my radar. But she was. Later, at a school dance marathon, I saw that same face flash by again.

Is that the girl from that time I saw Airplane!? I thought. It was—and once again, I couldn't take my eyes off her. I'd never talked to her before though, and I couldn't come up with a good way to start a conversation.

I kind of followed her around for a while in high school. Casual stalking, I guess you'd call it. I figured out her name: Melissa. I waited outside her drama class a lot, because I knew she would eventually have to exit out that door. I tried not to be too obvious about checking her out, though in later years, she would tell me that she could tell that I liked her—she just couldn't be bothered with a guy who couldn't even get it together enough to talk to her.

A little later, we both kind of failed school. While my own situation involved ditching class and punching a teacher, Melissa, I learned later, had struck a deal with her parents: If she got straight A's in her first semester of sophomore year, her parents would allow her to leave high school, get her equivalency certificate and move on to pursue art, her real interest, at junior college. Eventually, she went to cosmetology school.

I didn't know about any of that at the time, though. Instead, I just didn't see her anymore. Still, even after I got suspended, I had a weird feeling that my path and Melissa's would cross again.[13]

At that time in my life—the post-decking-a-teacher phase—I'd still hang out around the school, since it was a good place to meet people, even though I was barred from attending any classes. Once school let out, I'd go to my friend Bobby's place and get high, and I wouldn't show up at home for days on end. I'd only go home every once in a while to grab some clothes, and I always tried to do that while my dad was at work, so I wouldn't have to deal with (what I considered at the time to be) his judgmental bullshit.

Eventually, my parents decided they'd had enough. One of the times I swung by to get some things, I found that my parents had changed the locks. That night, I called Bobby.

"Listen, they changed the fucking locks on me," I said. "Can I crash at your place tonight?"

Bobby told me he was fine with it, but who knew what his dad would say. When I went over to Bobby's house that night, his dad never showed up—so it was cool.

Some nights I stayed with Bobby, but on other nights, I had to find other places to crash. My dad would park his motorhome in front of our house, so sometimes I would break into it and sleep there before getting the hell out before he woke up to go to work. Other times I would break into storage facilities, or into other peoples' empty motorhomes and sleep there. I tried to scrounge money, and if I had any extra after buying drugs, I would get a hotel room as a big splurge. When I couldn't find a place, I slept outside. On a few nights, I slept under a bush outside of a Long John Silver's restaurant. My first choice, though, was always Bobby's place.

Bobby[14] lived in this little 1,500 square foot house in Encinitas with his dad, who was an alcoholic bartender. His dad did his shifts during the day, and most nights, he would come home, lock himself in his room and drink all night—so, from our perspective, it was a pretty good place to party like crazy.

Once Bobby's dad had locked himself in his room, Bobby and I would invite people over. There was a downside to this, of course: everybody might have to scatter when Bobby's dad left his room or came home from work. Still, we knew that once he'd been home for a while, he'd lock himself in his room again, and we could start the whole process all over. Bobby's dad was partially deaf and way more than partially drunk—most of the time, anyway.

Bobby and I started selling drugs at these parties. We were also robbing people and stealing shit whenever we thought we could get away with it (which was fairly often). We were all about funding our own non-stop party, and the people who showed up were the people we sold to. We weren't out on the street looking for customers. We were selling drugs to our friends.

One of the drugs we sold—the leading product, in fact—was what we called crank, now better known as crystal meth.[15] We never smoked it or shot it, but we did snort a whole lot of it. Our lives kind of revolved around selling, using and eventually making crank.

Around the same time, I began experimenting with psychedelics: acid and mescaline and psilocybin. I took a lot of each and somehow never had a bad trip. I think it's because I always took psychedelics when I was with friends who were also taking them, in settings where I felt comfortable and safe. I remember actually being happy when I was around my friends and we were all tripping together. It was like we were all flying in the same sky, like we were the same people doing all the flying. I once dropped a lot of acid while reading Douglas Adams's *The Hitchhiker's Guide to the Galaxy*. I thought then, and now, that it was an important book—an essential piece of philosophy disguised as a comedic novel.

One of my big takeaways from *Hitchhiker* was that asking the right question was incredibly important. Other major lessons I got from the book: live and let live, do your best to minimize suffering and look for ways to honor your oneness with all other beings. It all sounds very intense and maybe even spiritual, I know. But regardless of whatever label you put on it, those were things I learned from Adams.

Over time, I got as into music as I was into comics. Even when I had no money, I would hang out at a record shop I loved until I got kicked out, then spend the other half of the day in the comic store (hoping I wouldn't get kicked out there, too). Those were my two happy places, and I spent my days between them. I didn't really have a job or direction otherwise, other than selling drugs. Then, one night at Bobby's house, Melissa showed up with her boyfriend, Frank, who was a buddy of mine. I was right: our paths had crossed again.

Frank introduced us, and we had to pretend like we'd never met before—though technically we really hadn't, since I'd never been able to start a conversation with her. Melissa became one of the people I did psychedelics with at Bobby's place, and we started talking and hanging out more. For a while, we were just really good friends…and then she broke up with Frank.

On our first "date,"[16] she took me to see *The Rocky Horror Picture Show*, which I am pretty sure was the world's first cult horror movie musical.[17] By taking me to that movie, Melissa gave me an amazing experience: some of the people in the audience had dressed up in costume to sing along with the songs in the film and shout dialogue and jokes that were better than the ones in the movie! Others were there to watch and listen to the people in costume, and—this was the cool part—*some* of the people in that movie theater audience were deeply confused civilians who had wandered in expecting it to be a regular movie. Melissa told me the people in this third group were known as *virgins*.

I already knew some of the songs, because Dr. Demento[18] featured the *Rocky Horror* soundtrack album pretty regularly on his weekly radio show, which I hardly ever missed. But the experience as a whole—the costumes, the singalongs and the making fun of virgins—took the music to another level.

Rocky Horror was the polar opposite of everything I had hated about high school: I felt safe, I was really high, I was with friends and we were making up our own rules. The show was a blast, especially the audience participation stuff. I loved the gasps from the virgins who hadn't expected anyone to shout through the film, and how people would throw rice and hot dogs at the movie screen or squirt water pistols in the air. Most of them figured they might as well go along with all the weirdness, and I loved that. It was a victory. *Rocky Horror* was subversive. It was fun. It was camp. In all, it was liberating.

About two-thirds of the way through that first screening, Melissa bit me on the neck to let me know that she liked me. My mind was officially blown at that point—and the rest of the night got even better. It was a wild night and a hell of a lot of fun.

We became boyfriend and girlfriend at that point, and Friday nights with Melissa at *Rocky Horror* became a tradition and the high point of the week. After every Friday night session, my face would hurt from laughing so much at all the things she said and did. Melissa and I were perfectly in sync, and we had the best time together. But it didn't take Melissa long to figure out that I was a terrible boyfriend.

At that time, I did whatever the hell I felt like doing whenever I felt like doing it. If that meant disappearing for days at a time and not telling Melissa (or my parents) where I was or what I was up to, that was not my problem. I had a busy schedule. I was stealing motorcycles and hanging out with metalheads and punk rockers; I fit her in when I could. The only structure to my life, really, was showing up on Friday night for the midnight show of *Rocky Horror*.

"Do you realize you never call me?" Melissa asked me one night. "That I wait by the phone for you to call and it doesn't ring? Ever?"

"Okay," I replied.

"That's it? 'Okay'? I don't think this is much of a relationship, Gary."

"Okay."

"Also, I think maybe you're heading down a bad road."

"Okay."

"As in, a road I don't particularly want to go down."

Melissa got high, but she never took anywhere near the amount of drugs that I did. She could tell what she was looking at.

I've forgotten the rest of the conversation; I was probably trying to forget it as it was taking place. The gist of it, though, was that Melissa gave me a choice: be with her, or continue doing whatever the hell I felt like doing whenever the hell I felt like doing it. When she saw I wasn't going to change any time soon, we broke up.

I was devastated, but I didn't feel like admitting that to myself or anybody else. So I did what I always did in times of stress: I got high.

The whole reason I got addicted to drugs is because they made me feel good and they gave me clarity. I was such a fucked up kid who'd had such a bad start that for most of my life, I didn't know what it was like *not* to feel like shit all the time. When I got high, I stopped feeling like shit. And, of course, I thought: *Oh, I like this.* Hell or high water, I didn't give a fuck—I was gonna get high. It was pretty much my life's goal at that point.

Melissa and I got back together a couple of times, but we would always eventually break up again. She didn't want to go down the same road I was heading down, but fortunately, we always still remained friends—really, really good friends.

One night, not long after another break up with Melissa, I was driving with Bobby in my awesome 1967 Oldsmobile. I'd bought it used with money I'd gotten from selling crank, and there were only 22,000 original miles on the thing. I told Bobby not to bring any of his shit with him, but he told me I was paranoid and brought it all anyway.

He was in the backseat with a scale weighing out methamphetamine when, of course, we got pulled over—why? Because I have a pair of toy Batman handcuffs hanging from my rearview mirror. When I saw the flashing red lights, it occurred to me too late that the rearview mirror maybe wasn't the best place for them.

I wasn't a complete idiot; I didn't want a high-speed chase or anything, so I pulled over, thinking maybe there was a way I could talk my way out of this. *Maybe not*, I thought immediately after checking the mirror. I couldn't believe my eyes: I *knew* the cop who was walking toward us.

"Shit," I muttered.

"What?" Bobby asked.

"It's Officer Petty."

Of all the cops in town, I had to get pulled over by *her*. We had a history. She had never liked me, and now, I had a bunch of meth in the back seat of my car. Shit was officially getting serious.

Officer Petty spotted me and smiled as she tapped on the driver's side glass. I rolled down the window.

"Hey there, Gary," she said.

She wanted me to call her by name, because we knew each other—and because she knew I'd have to say "Officer Petty" since I didn't even know her fucking first name. Instead of giving her the satisfaction, I stared straight ahead, giving her the silent treatment.

"Oh, it's going to be like that? Okay. You and your friend want to step out of the car, please?"

We did, and after she searched the car, she laughed like she'd just won the lottery. Bobby and I were both arrested and taken into the police station with our meth and drug paraphernalia—all thanks to toy Batman handcuffs.

After they separated us for questioning, Bobby ratted me out, making *me* look like the mastermind of the operation even though *he* was the guy in the backseat weighing everything out. After Bobby gave his statement, he pointed the finger at me and they let him go. I was screwed.

The Batman toy cuffs on the mirror were a misdemeanor, but the drug possession and the paraphernalia meant I was looking at a full-on felony. Not good.

After they put me in a holding cell, my dad came in furious, his eyes completely cold. Like the movies, each of us held a phone and talked to each other through a barrier of glass.

"You do realize how serious this is, right?" he asked.

"Yes, I do," I said. What else was I going to say?

"Listen to me, Gary, and listen very carefully: I know a good lawyer, and I'm going to call him. I'm going to handle this for you. Once. This *one* time and never again. But *you're* going to pay for it. You're going to sell that car of yours to pay for the lawyer. Understood?"

I gulp and say, "Yes. I understand." Again, what else was I going to say?

My dad got me his lawyer, I pled down to a misdemeanor possession charge and did four months in jail. After I got out, I saw Bobby again, and somehow, we worked it out. I never saw that sweet '67 Oldsmobile again, though.

In case you're wondering, my four months behind bars did not rehabilitate me—I'll fast forward and give you a highlight reel of how fast things started to get worse after I got out.

My thought process still wasn't great. If I needed money, I would go: *Okay, I'll steal some.* One time, my folks decided to let me stay with them again after I'd been up for seven or eight days straight high on crank. I knew I needed cash, and I also knew my neighbors had money. When my parents were out of town, I came up with a brilliant plan: I would break into the neighbor's place and steal a big glass water bottle full of pennies I knew they had after spotting it through their window. I figured there had to be at least a hundred bucks in there.

A buddy[19] and I broke into their house and grabbed that giant bottle full of pennies. We'd realized that we wouldn't be able to lift it over the fence, so we got a wire cutter, cut through the fence and pulled the bottle through. We might as well have put up a neon sign that said: *The Thieves Went This Way.* It was like we were auditioning for *America's Dumbest Criminals.*

I ended up losing a year of my life to that little scam, because I got busted again that night. I went back to county jail on my first felony charge. I was 19 years old.

Back in jail, the one thing I knew for sure was that I didn't want to be anybody's bitch. It didn't take long for me to get into a fight...and to lose it, because the guy hit me so fucking hard I went from upright to perpendicular in a fraction of a second, falling straight back and sending my glasses across the room. Flat out on the floor and looking up at the ceiling, I thought, *Man, that guy is really fast, and really strong...maybe I'll just stay down here.* I was surprised I had even remained conscious.

The sheriffs scraped me up off the floor and took me in to see the doctor, pouring me into a chair in the waiting area. Ten minutes later, the doctor showed up and sat on a stool right next to me, looking into my black eye to make sure it still worked (which it did, barely).

"So what happened?" the doctor asked. Of course, the two sheriffs were listening, waiting to see how I would answer the question. I didn't have to think very long before I answered.

"I slipped and fell in the shower."

Both of the sheriffs seemed skeptical, as did the doctor. "Really?" he asked.

"Yep," I replied. "Just went right down on my face. Crazy, you know?"

I'd already learned rule number one when I did my four months for possession: *Don't snitch.* So I didn't.

For the last six months of my sentence in county, I got sent to fire camp and was trained by the CDF to fight fires. Though they only paid a dollar a day, it was a dollar an hour, when during a fire—with the added perk of getting a steak for dinner.

I hated being locked up at night, but going out and fighting fires was something I actually enjoyed. I ended up getting hurt, though, because I fell off a mountain while fighting a fire and broke my tailbone, which sucked. Still, my last six months were actually kind of cool—and then I finally got out.

Now, you might think spending a year in county jail not doing crank would have given me some perspective. You might think the experience of doing physically hard work, being part of a team and helping people and communities that were in danger would have helped me at least *begin* to get my head straight. But you'd be wrong.

Shit was about to get even more serious.

PART TWO: BLACK MIRROR

In Part Two, I pull one burglary too many, get convicted of a felony, start doing time in prison, somehow get assigned the most dangerous cellmate the State of California has to offer, get sent to solitary confinement, and start going to AA meetings—for real, this time—when I finally get out. And as I start taking my own recovery seriously, I fixate even more on pop culture.

6. YOU PROBABLY WEREN'T EXPECTING THIS

People sometimes act surprised when I tell them that I have no regrets about going to prison. They look at me a little bit weird when I say that I wouldn't change a damn thing. They expect me to wish I could go back in time and do things all over again so I could make choices that *wouldn't* land me in prison.

But that's not how I look at it.

I look at it like this: That's where my life led me, and that's where I picked up some of my most important lessons. Prison isn't where I would recommend anyone *else* go for those lessons, but it's where *I* began to learn things. Why would I regret or want to change that?

Another thing I want to say about prison and the stupid choices that landed me there: I've never tried to conceal any of it. I'm open about sharing all of it, and I always have been. And there's at least three big advantages that come from owning up to your mistakes and sharing exactly what they cost you and what you've learned from them.

First, talking about your mistakes helps you connect with other people who can learn from them, and maybe become a little less likely to make the same ones in their lives—that's a huge part of what happens in recovery, by the way.

Second, owning up to your mistakes and being the first one to talk about them takes all the power away from people who think they can damage or destroy you by telling the world what you've done. See, there's no one who can blackmail me or hurt me by talking about my past. If someone calls me a felon, a drug dealer, a thief—you know what? They got that information from me, and I learned from those experiences.

And third, being open about your past—in a way that doesn't hurt other people—also gives you an important point of view about your own purpose in life.

We're human. We're all being taken places where we didn't expect to go or want to go. But wherever we're going, that's where we'll learn what we're supposed to learn next.

I'm grateful to prison, which is what this next section of the book is about, because of where it led me. Again, it's why I always say that I wouldn't trade prison for anything.

7. CRASH

CRASH[20] Golden Hill House is a halfway house in San Diego, or more technically, a "residential treatment service" program that "focuses on individual responsibility for recovery and productive re-entry into the community."

That wasn't how I thought of it at the time, though. For me, it felt a lot like being locked up.

CRASH was hardcore rehab, and it was way, way more intense than jail. It was designed to keep people out of prison by getting them started on the journey to recovery…and it was no bullshit. It was top-down, eyes-front, in-your-face stuff. When I first showed up at CRASH Golden Hill House in 1990, it was not something I wanted to do. It was something I *had* to do.

The program believed in radical behavioral therapy, and it was big on discipline, which meant it rubbed me the wrong way most of the time. For me, the experience was an extension of the whole how-do-I-get the-hell-out-of-here game at first, and I bet it felt that way for everyone who started the program.

Anyone who goes to CRASH is stuck in this big Victorian house for three months and can't even go outside. You start with no privileges and you earn more privileges as time goes on. After three months, if you play your cards right, you can win some time outside. You can't get high, which means being stuck in withdrawal, and you're not always happy about that. You're also given no room for error. You can't even set a foot wrong, and it's all recovery, all the time.

A lot of people look at a program like CRASH and ask one question: does it keep people from going to prison? Of everyone who goes in, how many end up going to prison—or *back* to prison? What is that percentage? I understand that perspective, and I do get why people would want to use a number like that to evaluate the program (I don't know what the numbers are, by the way.) But CRASH was an important part of my life and my recovery, *even though* I ended up going to prison after being in the program.

Did CRASH "fail" because I went to prison before recovery became anything like a real-world priority for me? I say no. CRASH was a beginning for me. It helped me to understand the mechanism of recovery, and it taught me a lot. It gave me the tools I ended up *using* in prison, which, believe it or not, is where I first got sober. (Side note: More people get sober and stay sober inside prison than a lot of people might imagine.)

CRASH taught me the 12 Steps of AA. As a 20-year-old with a radioactive personal history that I hadn't even begun to work through, I wasn't capable of following those steps…yet. But *learning* the steps and *trying* to follow them was an incredibly important part of the journey for me. More than that, CRASH got me out of my little suburban bubble for the first time. Where I grew up, there were white kids and Mexican kids and that was it. At CRASH, I lived with other men and women of all ages, makes, shapes and sizes, whether gay, straight or formerly homeless. CRASH opened my eyes to the reality that I lived in a world made up with a lot of people who had different backgrounds and points of view.

That said, I ended up bailing on the program after six months.

But here's the thing: Even after I left CRASH, I was still welcome at the meetings, and the people leading the meetings weren't judgmental when I showed up. They were just like, "I'm glad you're still coming to the meetings, Gary. Welcome back." And that was huge. *Wow, these are really forgiving people,* I thought. *They're really here to help.*

There were probably lots of people (besides my parents) trying to be kind to me as a kid and a young adult, but I was so fucked up that I couldn't even notice it, much less accept it. I didn't feel like I deserved it.

CRASH was the first place I actually noticed that there were people with basic human empathy.

At the time, I didn't feel normal. I didn't even feel human. I wasn't in school, and there was no structure in my life. I had been homeless, and I had been running. Half the time, I'd been running from drug deal to drug deal. It made a difference to get back to something that made me feel grounded, not like I was some street urchin. Something that made me feel like I was human, not a monster. Even though I quit eventually, CRASH made me feel like I belonged to something, which I hadn't expected when I started the program.

CRASH motivated me to try to do the right thing. For a little while. Until I started using again.

After that happened, I fell right back in with the old crowd, doing all the same insane shit. Every time I started using, I also started dealing—and each time that happened, a little voice in the back of my head said: *I'm gonna pay for all this someday. This is not something I'm gonna walk away from clean. I just know it.*

When I got out of CRASH, my parents took me back briefly, but they had one condition: I could not leave the house. They told me that if I snuck out, I should stay out. Of course, I still found a way to sneak out. I had a system.

My room was on the second floor, and I figured out a way to jump off of it and get out of the house without killing myself. I jumped off the balcony onto a little banister on the side and then jumped down from the banister. When I was coming back, I would just reverse the process (quietly, so I wouldn't wake my parents).

Usually, it all worked like a charm. But one night, I missed the banister, fell smack dab on the concrete and absolutely crushed my left hand. My buddy Bobby was waiting for me, because we were going to go out together. He'd seen what had happened and told me we had to go to the emergency room right away.

Bobby drove me out there, and when I arrived, I gave a false name. The doctors did what they could at the time and told me I'd have to come back to have my hand re-broken and reset. Since I was so paranoid about getting caught, though, I never went back.

Back at home, I pulled three of my knuckles hard and it hurt like hell, but it made it so my hand kind of worked again. My parents didn't find out, but my hand healed all wrong. I had always had a dream of becoming a lead guitar player in a rock band. *I guess that's gone now*, I thought—though I did start learning how to play bass.

8. THANK YOU, OFFICER

One night, while I was high, I decided that if I was going to keep living this life, I would need a gun—and suddenly, I had a great idea about how to get one.

What's so stupid about the part that comes next, the part that sent me to prison, is that it was totally, absolutely, completely, 100 percent pointless. I had all the drugs I needed, and I had about $3,000 in cash. I could have just kept all that in a safe place and had no problem with anyone. But I decided, *Hey, I want a gun. If I had a gun, I could walk around with my meth and my cash on me without feeling nervous. I could protect myself if shit ever got crazy. My ex-girlfriend's dad has a gun collection. I'm gonna go get myself a gun.* Great idea, right? If *you* were going to pick someone to steal a gun from, wouldn't *you* pick the father of an ex-girlfriend?[21]

There was no logical reason for any of it to happen. But unfortunately, it did.

That night, I broke into my ex-girlfriend's father's garage and immediately realized that this was *not* what I had wanted to do. *Shit,* I thought, as it dawned on me: *I forgot the gun collection is upstairs.* As I heard someone moving around upstairs, I realized that I wouldn't be able to pull off my plan. *I'm gonna have to abandon ship,* I decided—but as I was abandoning ship, this little fucking dog came out of nowhere and started barking at me with those extremely *loud* upper-register barks little dogs are so good at.

Okay, what do I do now? I thought. *Do I strangle the dog?* I decided that I wasn't about to kill this little dog; I was just going to leave.[22] I went back toward the little side door I'd broken into to get in the garage, but as I grabbed the handle, it just fell out of the fucking door. The door wouldn't open, and I could hear my ex-girlfriend's father walking down the steps of the house toward the garage. *Oh, boy.*

I looked around and decided my best option was to hide underneath his Porsche. I dropped down, scurried under the car and held my breath. Nothing happened for a second or two. Then, I saw his shoes. Next, my ex-girlfriend's father kneeled down, pointed a gun at me and said, "Get out. Stand up and put your hands on your head."

Shit—that's the gun I wanted, I thought as I crawled out from under the Porsche. *I fucking hate Porsches.*

A moment later, I was standing there with my hands on my head and a fucking gun pointed at me, close enough that I can see the bullets in the chamber. *Shit, I'm dead*, I thought. But he didn't shoot. Instead, and right away, lights started flashing outside, because the police had just arrived. *He must have called the cops before coming down here*, I thought.

The cops handcuffed me and took me away in the backseat of their squad car.

"You're lucky that guy didn't shoot you," one of them said. "You know who he is?"

I did, of course—he was my ex-girlfriend's dad—but whatever was coming next sounded interesting, so I said, "No, who is he?"

"He's a member of the official naval pistol team. He could have shot you between the eyes at a hundred yards."

"Yeah, well, he didn't need a fucking hundred yards," I replied—but inside, I was thinking: *Did this cop just save my life?* For maybe a minute, I was relieved to be alive. Then it sank in: *I'm in the back of a squad car. I'm under arrest.*

At that moment, I knew it like I knew my name: this was for real. *I've got a record, and it won't be jail or CRASH this time. This time, I'm going to prison.*

9. WELCOME TO THE MACHINE

With a criminal record already, I was now facing my second go-round with first-degree burglary. I'd been caught in the act, and there was no doubt about what was going to happen next. It was an open and shut case.

It was time for me to check into the criminal justice system once again—only this time, I was way over 18 and the ripe old age of 22. In my mind, of course, I was still a kid (and emotionally, I was frozen at about age five). But in the eyes of the law, which is what counted, I could be sentenced as an adult.

I was taken out to eastern San Diego to a place called El Cajon—basically a processing center—while waiting for my trial. Theoretically, you were only supposed to be at El Cajon for two weeks to a month at most, but I was there for four. It was either a sign of how bad the overcrowding was, how screwed up the computer system was or how terribly El Cajon was managed, but I never figured out which. What I can say is that El Cajon was not a good place to be stuck for four months.

It was kind of a Wild West situation. I figured out very quickly that, because El Cajon is an intake point, it was not designed as any kind of a permanent living setup. As a result, there were a lot of bad people around and a lot of rough stuff going on. Even the guards were high half the time, which meant people sometimes decided they could do whatever the hell they wanted, and you had to watch yourself.

Clearly, you didn't fuck around at El Cajon.

One day, I saw a guy I had partied with—a friendly face, right?—and sat down across from him at the lunch table. "Hey, Chuck," I said. He had no fucking idea who I was. He just stared at me like I wasn't there. Like *he* wasn't there. Later, I found out that he had murdered his girlfriend.

I started talking to some of the other prisoners, trying to figure out what kind of time I would likely have to do once I got to a real prison. Again, there's no doubt in my mind that, this time, prison really was where I'd be headed—and honestly, I'd seen it coming for a long time. My question was not: *How do I get out of this?* It was: *How bad is this going to be?*

"How many priors[23] you got, kid?" one of the inmates asked. I can't for the life of me remember his name, only that he looked a little like a walrus—but let's call him Gerald.

"One felony and a bunch of misdemeanors. Also some stuff that was dismissed."

"Okay. Tell me about those."

As I recounted, I had a lot of misdemeanors, and I'd had a lot of charges against me that had been dismissed. These were mostly possession charges; whenever I'd been busted for possession, it had always been for amounts that were so small that the judge didn't think it was worth prosecuting. This tells you two things: First, as much as I dealt drugs, I was fucking terrible at it. I was always using up the inventory myself. And second, I was ridiculously lucky. Every time I'd been busted for possession, I'd hardly had anything left after snorting or smoking my own product.

"Got it. And you're saying first-degree burglary is your felony prior conviction?"

"Yeah." I didn't mention that that was for boosting a big glass bottle full of pennies. I thought sharing that part of the story might damage my image at El Cajon.

"Don't worry about any of those possession charges," Gerald said. "They're too small to make a difference. When it comes to sentencing, the judge is going to set those aside. And don't worry about any of the misdemeanors, either. They won't figure into this. You've got one felony prior on the table, and that was when you were a minor. Here's what's going to happen. They'll offer you a deal. They'll probably offer you four years in exchange for pleading guilty. You should take it. If you do, you'll be out of wherever they send you in two years, assuming you don't do anything stupid. Every prison in California is jammed to overflowing. Give them some kind of evidence of good behavior, and you'll be back out in two years."

Ultimately, Gerald nailed it. That was exactly what ended up happening, and his advice probably saved my life.

The day I got sentenced in court was brutal. Both my mom and dad were there; he was cold and silent and she was crying her eyes out. I kept thinking: *Why the hell did they have to show up for this?* I didn't think I'd ever be glad to go back to El Cajon, but I actually felt relieved to get my four-year sentence so I could get away from them and back on the bus.

El Cajon was surrealistically overcrowded. There were six guys in a cell in some cases. There were four in mine, counting me, and Gerald was one of them. I was lucky that I had a decent bunch of cellies, and that no one in the cell hassled me. But you could tell the situation at El Cajon—the situation outside the cell—was unsustainable. There was just something in the air.

A prison break is pretty rare, but as it turned out, one of the biggest in San Diego history happened while I was at El Cajon. I saw it happen, though I never saw another one. It was a result of two things: overcrowding and incompetence. The overcrowding part makes human beings—any human being—even crazier than they may already be. And when it comes to crazy, it's fair to say that the folks in El Cajon (myself included) already had a pretty big head start on the general population.

In terms of incompetence, I learned later that the contractor the powers that be saw fit to hire to do some renovation screwed the city. These contractors put in a wall that was made out of stucco (as opposed to, I don't know, maybe reinforced concrete). Think about it: If you wanted to kick through a stucco wall, could you do that? I bet you could.

One night, I saw a bunch of prisoners bash a hole in a wall and make their way outside. I could have followed them, but I didn't; I figured I was already in enough trouble. That turned out to be a good decision, because all the guys who went through that hole in the wall ended up getting caught.

They shut down El Cajon over that incident, and we were all in lockdown for two weeks. Lockdown meant nobody could leave to take a shower and the guards brought crappy food to your cell—sparsely. If you're looking for a reason not to go into the correctional system, you could put "not eating enough" near the top of the list. At least, that's the way it was at El Cajon. We resorted to sucking down ketchup packets at one point just to get some calories and try to stop the hunger pangs, but it didn't help much.

We played Uno for two weeks, my cellies and me, sharing a toilet and trying not to notice how rank we all smelled. It wasn't easy, because by about day four, that cell was nasty. It only got nastier; the whole facility smelled foul, and I had never looked forward to a shower so much in my life. For that matter, I had never looked forward to three *other* guys taking a shower so much in my life.

Once we got out of lockdown, a guard showed up and informed me I had something I had to look forward to. The next morning, at the tender age of 21, I would be going to Folsom Prison. I took that in, shook it off as best I could, then noticed that Gerald and the other two guys were looking at me kind of funny—like they were sorry for me, almost, though there was a little bit of *Damn, I'm glad it's you and not me* mixed in with the expressions on their faces.

I sat up in my bed and looked at Gerald, who usually offered explanations in situations like this. But for the longest time, he didn't say anything. Finally, I shrugged, laughed like I wasn't scared of anything or capable of being scared of anything, and said, "What? What the fuck are you guys looking at?"

Gerald's eyes went sad on me. He shook his head and said, "Dude. You are going to gladiator school."

Folsom Prison. Johnny Cash had written a song about it and made an album there, but he definitely hadn't done any time there.

10. TWO WAYS TO BE SCARED

What Gerald said scared me from the top of my long-haired, bleach blond head down to the soles of my well-worn high tops, but I had learned already that showing weakness on the inside was not a good strategy for survival. Instead, I doubled down, pretending I was looking forward to gladiator school to hide the terror, exasperation and nausea I felt churning around in my stomach.

I wasn't hiding the fear as well as I thought, though, because that night, after the other two guys had gone to sleep and we could hear them both snoring, Gerald whispered to me from above. (He had the top bunk, and I had the lower bunk.)

"Kid—you awake?"

"Yeah."

"Listen. You've got a right to be scared. But you've also got a right to use it. They're making a big mistake sending you to Folsom. You're a level two. That means you should be going to a minimum security prison. But Folsom is full to the brim with level fours. It's a dangerous place. I'd be scared, too. But I'd *use* it."

Level twos were inmates like me—first-time incarcerated, convicted for things like burglary. Level fours were murderers, rapists, big-time drug dealers, Mafia guys—the ones who could make things difficult. Or make people dead.

"What do you mean, *use* it?" I whispered.

"Two ways to be scared, man. First way is you act tough, you pretend like you know everything and you don't do anything to protect yourself. Second way is you *use* fear. You make it motivate you. You *do* something about what you're scared of. You protect yourself. You make friends, for instance."

"Okay. I'm listening."

"So you want to know how to survive Folsom?"

"Of course, man."

"Then ask."

"How do I survive Folsom?"

"Rule number one: do not snitch. Under any circumstances."

I knew that one already. I told him about what had happened in the shower at Donovan, and how I'd handled it.

"Okay, good. Rule number two: don't pick a fight, but don't let people disrespect you, either. If you let one guy disrespect you and you don't draw the line and back it up right away, you're going to have problems. It's a balancing act, but you can figure it out. Don't stir shit up. Don't let someone fuck with you without consequences. Maybe the consequences turn out to be you getting your ass kicked, but that's better than you getting shanked. Clear?"

"Clear."

"Rule number three: mind your business. If it doesn't concern you, leave it alone. Clear?"

"Clear."

"Rule number four: stay out of the yard. If you don't have to go out there, don't go out there. Better to stay in your cell. Safer. Stay out of the gym, too. Clear?"

"Clear."

"Rule number five: don't fuck around with drugs. If you're going to get clean, prison is as good a place to get clean as anywhere. Remember, you can go to meetings, which are safer than the yard or the gym. Even if you don't have anything to say, it's better to go to a meeting than to go to the yard or the gym. Clear?"

"Clear—just like going to CRASH."[24]

"Right, just like going to CRASH. Rule number six: don't fuck with the gays. Don't hurt them, don't suck them off, don't get sucked off. Be polite, but steer away from them. Clear?"

"Clear."

"Rule seven. I know your folks send you stuff. Keep it that way. Stay on good terms with your folks if you can. Ask them to send you two things: books and cigarettes.[25] Clear?"

"Clear."

"Rule eight: don't fuck around with gambling. Don't give anyone else any crap for gambling, but don't you do it. Clear?"

"Clear."

"Rule nine: identify the level fours so you can stay the hell away from them. You can find somebody to help you with this. Probably a guard will help you out on this until you find somebody you trust. Guards know how fucked up it is to send a level two to Folsom in the first place. Clear?"

"Clear."

"Rule ten: make friends you can trust, and be there for them so they'll be there for you. Clear?"

"Clear."

"Rule eleven, last one: set up a routine of your own that you can follow no matter what else is going on. Follow it every day, and you won't go fucking crazy—that's the name of the game, by the way. Not going fucking crazy. Find something you can do exactly the same, every day. The routine you follow will keep you from going nuts. Clear?"

"Clear."

"Cool. That's how you survive Folsom."

There was a long silence. After a couple of minutes, I could hear him shifting around on the top bunk, trying to get comfortable so he could fall asleep, so I whispered.

"Thank you, Gerald. I wish to hell you were coming with me."

He laughed softly, then whispered: "Shut the fuck up and get to sleep. You've got a big day tomorrow."

11. THE MOST IMPORTANT HAIRCUT OF MY FUCKING LIFE

Early the next morning, I got loaded onto a bus with a bunch of other guys and we settled in for the longest motherfucking bus ride of my life: the ride to Folsom.

We were all chained at the ankles and the wrists. The ride was bumpy and slow and it just went on and on. I was on my way to gladiator school, and the only thing I could think about at the time was: *At least I get to smoke cigarettes again soon.* (My folks had sent me plenty of cigarettes—I guess by that point they knew that was basically currency inside—but there was no smoking on the bus.)

There was one brief stop, eight hours in or so, for a tiny and terrible lunch. The guards literally threw each of us a bag that had a baloney sandwich and a juice box in it, though by the time they threw that bag our way, we were all so hungry we would have eaten anything. I wolfed it down, still feeling hungry as the bus started up again. We kept on rolling down the road, bumpy and slow again. Nobody wanted us on the freeways, I guess.

Fourteen hours later, we finally pulled into Folsom Prison in the middle of the night. The bus stopped, and the guards unchained us and marched us in. Middle of the night meant that everybody was in their cell, so we all get paraded through in front of fucking everybody. *Great,* I thought. *I'm on display.*

I guess descriptions matter at this point, so I'll tell you that on this particular day of my life, I had very long blond hair and was wearing glasses—and only when I started walking off the bus did I think to myself: *This might not have been the best look for my first night at Folsom.*

As I walked through receiving with all the other guys who got off the bus, it occurred to me that because of my hair, I was probably the single easiest person in the whole group of fresh meat newcomers to spot and remember. As I made my way through the line, I heard one guy shout: "Hey Goldilocks, you wanna taste of my sack lunch?"

The whole place erupted in laughter, and not the good kind. The kind of laughter that said: *Everyone now has permission to mess with Goldilocks.* What the hell had I gotten myself into? I kept walking, looking straight ahead, and made a mental note to myself: *No matter what it takes, I need to get a fucking haircut—now.*

The operative word was *now*, because if any situation was urgent, this one certainly was. I knew I couldn't wait until I had connected with someone I trusted enough to say, "Hey, nice to meet you. Listen: I need a quick haircut. Do you think maybe you could find some way to make me look like I'm not, you know, um, Goldilocks?"

Fortunately for me, a guard with intense eyes happened to be leading our group into a holding area. Intense Eyes looked like he'd seen it all before and had decided he'd seen just about enough—but from the expression on his face as he looked at me while everyone laughed, I got the sense that, as jaded as he was, he knew what the stakes were for me and he didn't particularly want me to get killed.

I decided it was time to throw the dice.

As we filed into the holding area, I leaned over to Intense Eyes and asked him, quietly, "Man, is there a pair of scissors in the place?" I kept right on walking, but I maintained eye contact. He looked right through me, sizing me up like he was sizing up the entire prison by. After a few seconds, he looked away, then whispered something to another guard.

After the other guard whispered something back, Intense Eyes walked away—purposefully enough to make me think he might not be ignoring me. That he might actually know where to find a pair of scissors and might be willing to save my ass. It was a lot to hope for, but I had nothing else. It wasn't like any of the guys who had come in on the bus were going to be carrying a pocket knife or a pair of shears.

Maybe three minutes later, Intense Eyes reappeared, walked over to me and handed me a pair of scissors. "You owe me, Buechler," he said. "Make sure I don't regret this."

I nodded, thanked him and started doing the job myself. A few of the other guys started laughing as they watched me clip away my Goldilocks as fast as I fucking could. Nothing about the situation seemed funny to me, though.

I'd only gotten about 90 seconds into the self-barbering, though, before another guard walked into the holding room. This one is big, built like a bull. For some reason, he immediately strikes me as a psychopath.

"PHOTO TIME, ASSHOLES, LINE UP HERE!" Psycho Bull shouts—then spots me cutting my hair, shoots me a look, slaps me on the side of the head and grabs my scissors. Yep: psychopath.

With that, we all got marched off to another room to get our pictures taken.

The good news was I no longer looked like Goldilocks. The bad news? With my wire-rimmed glasses and half-and-half haircut, I looked like 1968-era John Lennon in the midst of a severe personality crisis. Intense Eyes was kind enough to notice this, and from the back of the room he shouted, "Hey, check out John Lennon!"

Right as the prison photographer immortalized the moment for posterity, everyone in the room laughed except Psycho Bull. The nickname stuck: instead of Goldilocks, I was John Lennon. Thank God.

After the photos, I lit up a cigarette and took a deep drag as soon as I could. That nicotine hit had been a long time coming.

12. I IGNORE GERALD

A couple of words are in order about why Intense Eyes[26] was willing to make things easy for me:

He knew I shouldn't have even been at Folsom in the first place, because I was a Level Two. Theoretically, Old Folsom—the original facility, where I had landed—was for Levels Three and Four. A severe prison overcrowding situation in California had caused the Bureaucrats-In-Charge to cut some corners, causing a lot of Level Twos like me to get thrown into the lion's den. I guess Intense Eyes figured the odds were already stacked high enough against me.

I'd caught a break, and don't think I didn't know it.

Eventually, I found a barber—an inmate who knew how to cut hair—who was willing to fix the disaster of a "haircut" I'd given myself. The price? A pack of cigarettes. It was expensive, but it was the best available option. Life in Folsom, like life everywhere else, was all about picking the best available option.

In Folsom, I learned that life isn't made up of black and white. It's made up of a lot of different shades of gray—but the thing is, the grays can get a hell of a lot darker than usual in places like this one. I was terrified on Day One, and I stayed terrified for a long time.

Folsom was a scary place. It was a violent place. It looked like fucking Alcatraz, which I had seen once; my parents and I had visited it as tourists when I was 10 years old. This place had that same weird vibe of being ancient, haunted, determined that you respect its capacity to fuck you up. It wouldn't let you forget how many lives it had destroyed, and how yours could be the next one. Folsom was old and falling apart and its Level Fours were not to be fucked with.

People got killed. I saw fights between groups of seriously crazy men break out in the yard; I saw people get shot by the guards first with rubber bullets—then, with real bullets. I saw one guy shot right in the head, dead, and I watched him go down. I knew at that moment that I had to be on my guard 24/7 if I was going to survive. I also knew, from that day forward, that I had to follow Gerald's advice not to go in the yard if I could possibly find a way not to.

You might be wondering why I went out into the yard in the first place when Gerald had warned me not to. Simple answer: I was so eager to get some time away from my celly, Kyle,[27] that I thought I might as well risk a session out there, just to see what it was like. Well, I found out.

After I saw that guy get his brains blown out, I made myself a promise: *Never again.* I would be staying in my cell until I came up with some better plan. Unfortunately, that meant more face time with Kyle.

Usually, I didn't consider myself someone who did a whole lot of praying, though that had changed right after I learned I was headed to Folsom. My experiences with psychedelics had opened me to the possibility that there might be something more to life than I'd expected, something that matched up with what most people called God. Something that connected everything and made it easier to ask the right questions—whatever name that something ended up having.

I knew what was going on in church was bullshit, and if you'd asked me if I believed in the God most people talked about, I would have said no. But I also had a gut feeling that there was something deeper, some purpose to all that I was going through. Suddenly, I was ready to be the kind of person who prayed to...whatever.

And what was I praying for? That I'd get assigned a celly who wouldn't freak me out, wouldn't mess with my head, wouldn't make me feel anxious in my own bed.

That very first week in Folsom, I got fresh evidence, as if I needed any, that not all prayers get answered. Because after the guards led me in, locked the cell door and walked away, the first thing five-foot four, 300-pound-plus, bald-as-a-cueball Kyle Freedy said to me from the bottom bunk was: "Please tell me it's not *fucking* true that you pulled a four-year sentence. Please tell me the guard was *fucking* lying to me about that to mess with my *fucking* head."

No *hello*. No *nice to meet you*. No *I'm Kyle, what's your name?* Just a request that I tell him that the sentence I'd been given…wasn't the sentence I'd been given. For a couple of seconds after he said it, I was too confused to speak. Mostly, I was trying to figure out why the hell he was staring at a spot about two feet to my right, like I had someone standing next to me.

"Well?" Kyle pressed. He seemed to expect an answer, but he was still staring at a person beside me who wasn't there.

"Um…yeah, I'm supposed to get out in four years. Two if I keep my shit together, I mean. Which I, you know, really want to do."

His eyes—blue-grey, empty and cold—had darted right toward my face the instant I started talking. They kept staring me down like they'd never seen a face before. After a couple of seconds, I figured it out: *This guy's blind.*

"Jesus Christ, listen to you. *Young*, too. Your whole *fucking* life ahead of you. Right? Right?" His face twisted into a scowl. "*Right?* Buechler?"

"I, uh—yeah, I guess so."

"How old, exactly." He spat the words out. It didn't even sound like he was asking questions anymore. Just mad at me for being young. (He looked to be in his late 40s.)

"Twenty-two."

"Twenty-*two*. Fuck you. You *guess* so. And you aim to keep your *shit* together. For *two years*. And start *over*. *Fuck* you."

I stood there, mentally replaying what had to be the strangest conversation I had ever had in my life, trying to figure out the safest way to get up to that top bunk. It seemed a bit of a risk to just start climbing up the ladder, because that would definitely be ignoring him. As bad of a start as this was, I didn't want to make it any worse. Finally, I decided to ask him a question.

"How long are you in for?"

He acted like I hadn't said anything at all. He just stared straight ahead. I had no follow-up question, and he had no response. He just kept staring me down with those empty eyes. After what might have been five minutes, I decided it had to be safe to climb up onto the top bunk. When he heard me move, he looked away.

I settled into the bunk and nothing changed. He didn't say a word to me for the rest of that night. The next morning, one of the guards told me he was in for life. He'd murdered two kids my age during an argument over whose turn it was to buy heroin, and he'd eaten their lunch next to their dead bodies.

It went on like that. For days. Dead silence. Then, abuse.

After about a week of Kyle Freedy's psycho-ward, head-trashing bullshit, I needed to change the pattern. I figured things probably couldn't get much weirder with Kyle, so I might as well give the yard a test drive and check out the weirdness quotient there, despite what Gerald had told me. What was I, a pussy? I needed to see for myself. Which turned out to be a mistake.

Not only was I wrong that it could get a *hell* of a lot weirder in the yard than in my cell, I also knew that if I went out there again, I might be the next guy who caught a bullet or got shanked for breaking some rule I didn't know existed. If not that, then I'd get set up in some other way—because, let's face it, I was an easy target.

Bottom line: it was time to stay the fuck out of the yard. No exceptions, end of story, just like Gerald said. I would have to put up with Kyle's head games, no matter how much they messed me up.

13. HOW NOT TO GO INSANE

My shoulders and back stiffened up like planks. I started having nightmares. Then, I started worrying about what I might be saying in my brief snatches of sleep that could possibly give Karl material he could use to fuck with me the next day.

If I'm honest, the whole sleeping thing became a big problem, one that got bigger with each passing day and made other problems bigger, too. If you've never had to "sleep with one eye open," never had to worry about being attacked in the middle of the night by someone in the same room who hates you and has a documented history of violence, I hope you never do. It's a horrible experience.

Now, you might well ask why the hell the system had put a first-timer like me in with a seriously crazy bastard like Kyle Freedy. This question certainly crossed *my* mind many times. Old Folsom, the rat-trap of an institution where I landed, was meant to be for Level Three and Level Four inmates. Well, Kyle Freedy was about as Level Four as Level Four got. If there had been a Level Five, he wouldn't have had to audition for it.

Remember how I said a lot of Level Twos like me had been shunted into this hellhole that absolutely, positively wasn't meant for us in any way, shape or form? Well, I found out later that one of the core principles of the state of California's (and America's) penal system design is that you don't put a Level One or a Level Two inmate in the same cell as a Level Three or a Level Four. Overcrowding problem or no overcrowding problem. It's just not done.

It's a mistake, like malpractice if you're a doctor or lying to a judge if you're a lawyer, which gets you expelled from the bar. You don't ever want it to happen, under any circumstances, and there's a good reason for it: people get killed in that situation. Even so, there were hundreds of us Level Twos in Old Folsom sharing our bunk space with Level Three and Level Four cellies.

The answer to my question was pretty depressing: System? What system? There was no longer any System to speak of. The Powers That Be either didn't care what the fuck happened to us, or—and this was the really interesting scenario if you leaned toward being paranoid, which at that point in my life, I definitely did—they thought this was some kind of cool social experiment. Maybe they were curious. Maybe they wanted to find out just how long it would take a Level Two—me, let's say—to get chewed up and spit out like bad meat. Maybe they had an office pool on it or something.

That sounds nuts as I write it down, so do I believe it now? Of course not. Did I believe it on a mad night on that top bunk, sleep-deprived and spiraling, knowing that I was locked in a room with a maniac and would have to stay locked up with him for the foreseeable future? Maybe. And maybe you would have, too.

Lots of people have asked me why Kyle Freedy, who clearly hated my guts the instant I walked into that cell and made sure I remembered how much he hated me every single fucking day, didn't just shank me while I was sleeping. I've given this question a lot of thought, and I've come up with two explanations that might explain the mystery. Maybe they both do.

First reason: If Kyle Freedy killed his celly, he knew he'd end up in the hole for a very long time. He hated the hole, and he spent a lot of time explaining exactly what he'd do to me if I ever did anything that sent him there.[28]

The other reason I didn't get shanked, as I see it, was pleasure. Frankly, I think Kyle enjoyed knowing he was scaring the shit out of me. I think it calmed him down somehow. After a while, he decided it would be fun to transition between being nice to me, *then* scaring the shit out of me, just to mix things up.[29] This was recreation for him.

Another big question I always get is how I stayed sane in a situation like that. Two answers here: First, I remembered what Gerald had told me, which I'm repeating verbatim below for the sake of anyone who happens, for whatever reason, to find themselves in a similar situation at Folsom or anywhere else. If that's you, please write these words down and tape them to a mirror, or to some other surface you are likely to see every day:

Set up a routine of your own that you can follow, no matter what else is going on. Follow it every day, and you won't go fucking crazy. That's the name of the game, by the way: not going fucking crazy. Find something you can do exactly the same every day. The routine you follow will keep you from going nuts.

My second answer to the question, which I think is just as important as the first one? **Comic books and graphic novels.**

So, after my one trip to the yard, with the exception of meals and the occasional scheduled trip to the library or the prison store (yes, prisons have stores), I stayed in my cell and did my damnedest to tune out Kyle Freedy.

My go-to option for doing that was reading, and my go-to reading material was comic book anthologies and graphic novels. Folsom rules said people couldn't mail you floppy comic books—don't ask me why. Any book you received in the mail had to have a spine. So...comic books in book form, please. That's what I put on my wish list, even though I saw how a lot of inmates and their relatives had figured out ways to smuggle traditional comic books into Folsom.

There was another good reason to focus on anthologies and graphic novels, a reason that had nothing to do with following prison rules: the plots were self-contained. There were cliffhangers, sure, but in anthologies, you were always looking at standout stories that stood the test of time and were worth reading on their own merits. When it came to graphic novels, you always got a complete character arc. I figured there was no sense getting hooked on an individual comic book's storyline when there was no way to guarantee that I'd be able to get hold of the next month's issue.

My allies in maintaining this lifeline were my parents. In addition to replenishing my store account whenever I needed it, my mom and dad sent me an endless supply of reading materials based on a written list I updated regularly. And let me tell you: I burned through that list. The very first item on it, a book I not only devoured but kept coming back to, was *The Greatest Joker Stories Ever Told,* an anthology of classic DC Joker versus Batman stories collected over almost half a century.

I'm not going to lie, the Joker was a big deal for me. There was something important, something worth exploring, about a guy who managed to survive, thrive, break out of prison and leave his mark on a world where chaos and disorder was the name of the game. Those Joker stories spoke to me at a deep level, and they got me through some tough days. This was entertainment, yes, but it wasn't *just* that. This was survival, and I did a lot of survival reading in that top bunk.

Some people will tell you that the Bible got them through a prison experience. If I had to pick a set of scriptures that worked for me during this part of my life, it would maybe be rereading Tolkien like the Old Testament (I had inhaled *The Lord of the Rings* at an early age), while the DC stories pitting the Joker against Batman-slash-the-Dark-Knight would stand in for the New Testament. Those were the scriptures I kept coming back to. Frank Miller's *The Dark Knight Returns* was another important piece of survival reading.

My parents knew how important this stuff was to me, and despite all that I had put them through, they never failed me—not once. They kept the care packages coming like clockwork, twice a month. I got a steady stream of them, all assembled by my mom, who included a letter with whatever she sent.

It was something Kyle Freedy noticed and mentioned, and not necessarily in a good way. It was more in a kind of creepy way. For instance: "Another package from *Mom*? Aren't *you* lucky." I got a break from Kyle during mealtimes, of course, and I don't mind telling you that I looked forward to them.

I don't know how it is now, but back then, Folsom was as segregated as segregated got. You saw it at mealtimes, and you also saw it in the way cellmates were assigned. A white inmate always got a white inmate as a celly, a Black inmate always got a Black celly, a Mexican inmate always got a Mexican. The prison officials believed that segregating the prisoners by race would make race riots go away, but that didn't work—I saw and steered clear of multiple race riots while I was there.

Still, the fact that segregation didn't eliminate racial violence didn't change the policy. Everything was set up according to what race you were, and that definitely applied to meals. At Donovan and El Cajon, there were plenty of times when I sat down with an inmate who was Black or Mexican and we would talk together, play backgammon, whatever. That just didn't happen here. You'd probably survive, but why risk it? So, I sat and ate with white inmates.

Eventually, though, I always had to head back to that cell. Every time I got there, Kyle Freedy was either walking with me, waiting for me or about to show up. Which is why every time I got there, I grabbed a book, climbed up to the top bunk and started reading.

Thanks to the money my parents kept depositing in my store account, I was able to buy a small tape player and AM/FM radio for the cell. It surprises a lot of people that I was able to do this, but I was. Even a nightmare like Folsom lets you have certain basic amenities, assuming you can pay for them.

The first night we had the damn thing in the cell, though, at about two in the morning, not caring whether or not I was asleep (I wasn't), Kyle said to me, "Your *mom* bought me a *tape player,* Buechler."

I pretended I hadn't heard him.

14. THE PRUNO INCIDENT

To understand this next part, you need to know what pruno is. If you already know what pruno is, bear with me while I brief the civilians.

Pruno is what happens when prison inmates decide to make alcohol out of whatever ingredients they've been squirreling away while the guards aren't looking—fruit, fruit juice, potatoes, sugar, bread, even hard candy. If you were in a generous mood, you could call the end result "wine", but a better and more accurate description might be what a journalist in California called it: "bile-flavored wine-cooler."

In terms of its ability to get you drunk, pruno is a crap shoot. The alcohol content veers from about two percent (think light beer) to about 14 percent (think Cabernet Sauvignon), and you never know which alcohol level is going to show up. It tastes like Tang that's been left behind a radiator for a couple of weeks. Sometimes, it can get you drunk, but surprise, surprise: it's dangerous. Plenty of cases of botulism are linked to pruno.

I knew all that from my time in El Cajon, which was why even after months away from my usual sources of supply for things like beer, weed and crank, I chose to stay away from the stuff. Kyle Freedy, on the other hand, was a major fan. He was brewing a big batch of pruno in a black plastic bag under his bed, and he shared the stuff with his buddies. There was a clandestine pruno network at Folsom, and he was part of it.

So why do I tell you all this? Because one morning, Kyle was out in the yard lifting weights[30] and I was all alone in the cell, enjoying being all alone for a change. I looked in my mirror and I saw a bunch of guards—

the search team. They were going from cell to cell, and my best estimate was that they were going to be in *this* cell in about two minutes.

I'm gonna get the fucking blame for all this pruno, and so is he, I thought. *Kyle and his buddies can always make some more.* So, I dumped the pruno into the sink, turned on the tap, and washed it all away, quickly. It was disgusting. When the guards came in, they searched, found nothing and left.

Fifteen minutes later, Kyle Freedy came back in from the yard, and I explained what happened. He looked at me like I was a bug he wanted to step on but couldn't yet, for reasons he couldn't be bothered to share.

"Buechler," he said, "you're going to have to pay for that pruno." Everybody else called me John Lennon, but with this guy, it was always Buechler.

Kyle and I had very different views of what had just happened. My view was that I'd just kept both of us from spending a couple of days in the hole, which is no one's idea of a good time. Kyle Freedy's view was that I threw out his kicker—the fermented fruit goop that's kind of like a starter for sourdough bread, because it gets passed from batch to batch—when I should have found some way to keep the guards from discovering it. It was fucking ridiculous, because I'd had two minutes, tops, and the search teams find things because it's their job—but I digress.

The point is, Kyle pressed the issue. He thought he had an angle. He thought he'd figured out a way to secure some kind of tangible advantage out of the joke the universe played on him by making him live with a 22-year-old kid who would probably be out of Folsom in two years. So he doesn't agree to disagree.

"Buechler, now hear this," he said instead. "I'm not backing down on this, motherfucker. You need to put twenty bucks in my book." He meant his account at the prison store. "I don't care how you do it—write your mom a nice letter, do whatever you need to do, but get that twenty in my book."

We went back and forth on this for hours before I finally caved. I agreed to put 20 dollars in his book, imagining that it would make the problem go away. Which, of course, it didn't.

The day after I put the twenty dollars in his book, he waited until about midnight to say word one to me. I was up on the top bunk, trying and failing to get to sleep. I was spiraling yet again when I hear him say: "Actually, Buechler, that kicker was worth way more than what I charged you. I need you to put another twenty bucks in my book."

I pretend not to hear him. So he climbs halfway up the ladder, shakes me by both legs, and says: "Buechler. You need to put another twenty bucks in my book, man."

Like an idiot, I thought he'd appreciate how I was doing him a favor by dumping the pruno and keeping him out of the hole. Then he'd gotten in my face about that, and like an idiot, I'd thought that if I pretended like the two of us had stumbled into some kind of gray area and I was giving him the benefit of the doubt, he'd shut the fuck up for a day or two. But he didn't. Here it was, the very next day, and he was at it again. At this point, while that bastard was shaking my legs and calling my bluff, I knew damn well Kyle Freedy wasn't *really* talking about pruno.

This asshole was—to use some prison language that the civilians reading this may or may not be ready for, but too bad, because there's no other way to put it—out to make me his bitch.

That's what was going on here. He knew it and I knew it. That's what he was visualizing behind those blind, dead eyes: me as his bitch. He wanted me to do one of two things: become his slave, or snap and do something stupid, so I'd have to spend more time in Folsom.

It wasn't a great set of options, but I knew this insane problem I'd found my way into was only going to get worse—a thousand times worse, with Kyle Freedy and with everyone else— if I let him bitch me out.

And here's the big life lesson I learned from Kyle Freedy, of all people: this shitty, impossible situation may not have been my "fault", but dealing with it was my responsibility. And so far, I'd been fucking it up.

In fact, the more I thought about it, the clearer it became to me that getting stuck inside this problem in the first place had a hell of a lot more to do with me than it did with him. I had let myself be disrespected. He'd disrespected me from the moment I'd walked into that cell, and I'd let it stand. He'd disrespected me when he'd made that crack about my mom buying him the tape player, and I'd said nothing. He'd disrespected me when he'd demanded that I write a letter to my parents to send me extra money so I could put it in his book, and I'd gone ahead and done it like a fucking idiot. He was disrespecting me right now by shaking my fucking legs and upping the ransom. I hadn't drawn the line on any of it. I'd let it all slide.

Why? Because part of me, deep down, believed that I didn't really belong here. That I was out of my element at Folsom. Eventually, I'd be able to explain that to someone in charge. Push my glasses back up to where they belonged after they'd drifted down, raise an index finger, and say, "Excuse me. I think there's been some mistake. I'm really not supposed to be in this situation." And it would somehow all get fixed. I'd wake up somewhere else.

But I *was* here. This *was* Folsom. I *wasn't* going to wake up any place different. There *was* nobody in charge if I wasn't in charge. And whether I liked it or not, if I was going to survive, I was going to have to survive the way guys in Folsom survive.

I looked over my shoulder, stared Kyle Freedy in his dead eyes and said, "Fuck you. I'm not putting any more money in your goddamn book. And get your hands off me, motherfucker."

The good news? He gave a little smile, let go of my legs and climbed back down the ladder.

The bad news? Once he had settled into his own bed, he shouted, loud enough for the whole cell block to hear: "GAME ON, BUECHLER. GAME ON."

15. SEEK AND DESTROY

The next couple of days were pretty intense.

Kyle Freedy kept finding new ways to try to bitch me out, and I kept telling him to fuck off. He kept giving me that little smile that said, "This isn't over," and the cycle kept repeating. Looking back, I think he was trying to get me to make the first move, because a) he wanted to be able to claim he hadn't started anything, get me into trouble and lengthen my sentence, and b) he thought he could take me. I thought he could, too. He was short and heavy, yeah, but he had massive arms. Whatever his thinking was, he had made fucking with me his special project.

For about three days straight, after I told him I wouldn't be putting any money in his book, he gave me every possible excuse to slug him.

One afternoon, I was playing Metallica's "Seek and Destroy." This was during a daily slot that we'd agreed I could play music on my tape player. (Routine, right?) After my slot was over, Kyle Freedy could choose a tape—from my collection, by the way, since he didn't have any—that he wanted to hear. While I was listening, the bastard walked over, punched the STOP button on the tape player and said, "New rule: no Metallica."

I glared at him, picked up the tape player, brought it up to my bunk, and hit the play button again. As "Seek and Destroy" played, I shouted, "New rule, motherfucker: no new rules."

This kind of stuff kept happening. He kept poking at me, seeing if I'd go back to letting him get away with shit. He never, ever gave up, and I knew he never, ever would. Why not? Two reasons.

Reason Number One hadn't been on my radar screen until the you-owe-me-20-more-bucks thing: he really was nuts. I don't mean "crazy" like when you say, "Oh, so-and-so is crazy sometimes." I mean *crazy*. Seriously mentally ill.

Reason Number Two was almost as good, and was very, very familiar by now: he just flat-out hated my guts. He hated that I would be getting out before he would, because he knew *he* was never getting out. He hated that I could start over and he couldn't. And if he couldn't make me his bitch, he at least wanted to make damn sure I couldn't start over.

16. THE SHOEBOX INCIDENT

One day, I came back to the cell after taking a shower. As the guard let me in, locked the gate behind me and walked away, I glanced at the bottom bunk. My blood froze.

Kyle Freedy had found and opened up the shoebox I kept my letters from home in. He was sitting on his bed and going through my mail.

"I like your mom's handwriting," he said, without looking up.

Jesus Christ, the bastard is blind! It was absurd and terrifying at the same time. The room was already starting to get a little wobbly.

"Buechler, I want you to write your mom a letter," he continued. "I want you to tell her she should write me. I want to hear that letter before it goes out."

I could hear a weird ringing in my ears. It was growing louder by the second.

"Fuck no, you're not getting a letter from my mom," I said. "Get out of my shit. And give me that fucking shoebox, right now."

Kyle Freedy looked up—if that's what you can call what a blind guy does when he points his face at yours but doesn't quite catch up with where your eyes are—and said, "You're writing that letter. You hear me, Buechler?"

I was scared to death, but I knew what the score was. This was going to be a fight. This was a situation where *somebody* got the shit kicked out of them. My wheels were spinning. *This guy's blind, but he's bigger and stronger than I am*, I thought. *He works out a lot, and he's certifiably insane. A good outcome here is that I don't die. A good outcome here is that I just get my ass beat really, really bad. But there has got to be a fight, and it has to happen now.*

That part was non-negotiable.

"Buechler?"

The ringing in my ears was getting worse. *Okay, the louder the fight, the better my chances*, I reasoned, *because the sooner the guards hear that something's going down, the sooner they show up to stop the fight before somebody gets killed. And then maybe, assuming I'm not dead, I get out of this fucking nightmare and get a different celly who isn't Charles Manson 2.0.*

All I could hear was the ringing in my ears. Kyle Freedy's mouth wasn't moving anymore, but if it were, I don't think I would've been able to hear him. *Do it now—get the jump on him*, I said to myself. *It's the only advantage you've got.*

Quickly, I reached up into the top bunk and grabbed the tape player. Yanking the cord out of the back, I lunged at Kyle Freedy and started swinging it.

Tape players were big and heavy back then, so when it caught him across the nose, it knocked him right off his bed and onto the floor.

"You're not getting a letter from my fucking *mom!*" I screamed at the top of my lungs—partly because I needed the guards to hear, but partly, let's face it, because I was off the chain at that stage.

I belted him hard across the bridge of his nose again with that tape player for a second hit, beginning to lose my shit. Kyle was moaning.

"No *fucking* way! No letter from my *mom*, asshole! You hear *me? Huh?*"

Kyle was unconscious, and I had his blood all over me, but I figured: *One more for good measure.* I clocked him on the side of the head as hard as I could, just to make sure he gets the message.

"No *fucking* letter from my mom!"

My voice was hoarse and cracking under the strain of shouting so loud.

Finally, the guards showed up—I hadn't even heard them come in—grabbed the tape player and shoved me to the ground, hard. One of them sat on my chest and leaned his forearm across my throat, which hurt like hell. I could hear the other guard slapping Kyle Freedy, trying to wake him up.

I had never been so happy to be restrained by a man in uniform in my entire life.

17. WHY I DIDN'T GO IN THE HOLE

I didn't kill the guy, but I did earn a reputation as a badass, which, let me tell you, was not my intention going in. This was supposed to be about survival.

I was not aiming to get anyone's attention—except maybe the guards, so they'd show up sooner rather than later and the asshole wouldn't kill me. But for the next day or two, apparently the whole place was buzzing with stuff like:

"*Damn,* John Lennon went fucking crazy on Freedy."

"John Lennon sent Freedy to the infirmary."

"John Lennon busted Freedy's nose with his fucking tape player."

You might well ask, as a lot of people would: What kind of punishment did I get for that little adventure? Answer: One day in solitary. Not, say, 30 days in the hole, which was what I was expecting.[31] Frankly, it was a ridiculously light response to one guy knocking out another guy and breaking his nose. Why the light sentence? I've got my theory.

Right after the fight, they split the two of us up, which was standard, and told me I had to spend a day in solitary. They put me in a little cell where I spent the next day alone, but I could still hear everything going on elsewhere in the cell block. I still had my books and my letters—believe it or not, I even had my tape recorder, the one my parents sent me, and all of my tapes. I had to wash some of Kyle's blood off of it, but honestly, it sounded better to me than it had before I'd bashed him with the thing. When it was time to eat, I even got to go to the cafeteria.

I should probably explain the difference between "solitary" and "the hole." Solitary is nothing compared to the hole. At least I had my copy of *The Dark Knight Returns* in solitary. In the hole, you've got no books. You've got no contact with anyone, not even the guard who brings your food. They slide the tray with the food through a little opening near the floor. No face to look at, no voice to hear except your own. You just sit there, totally cut off from the rest of humanity. It's literally torture. If you doubt that, google the phrase "solitary confinement united nations" and look at what comes up.

Torture or not, 30 days in the hole was technically what was supposed to happen to you if you busted somebody's nose in Folsom and the guards saw you doing it. That was my situation. And I didn't get 30 days in the hole. Basically, I got a slap on the wrist.

As I did my day in solitary, which still sucked, I was getting more and more curious about something: Why the light punishment? Was it my pretty face? My great relationship with prison guards and administrators? My supposed resemblance to the late, great John Lennon?

Nope. I'd gotten a slap on the wrist for one reason and one reason only: the guys who ran Folsom Prison knew that they had fucked up.

What the hell was a Level Two inmate (think Ferris Bueller, but with an attitude and a fucked-up childhood) doing in the same cell with a Level Four inmate (think Charles Manson overlapping with Jeffrey Dahmer)?

That was the question The Powers That Be were doing their level best to make sure nobody started asking. Despite the best efforts of The Powers That Be, my parents *did* ask that question, loud and clear, to whoever would listen to them. They got nowhere—but they were the only ones asking it.

18. THE PLAN

After one day in solitary with the Dark Knight and the Joker to keep me company, I got assigned to a new celly—Level Two—named Liddle Pepper, an old homeless guy from San Francisco with long, thinning, straggly gray hair. He was in his mid-50s or so, and he'd been around. He had five more years to serve for breaking and entering.

I was pretty quiet for the first few hours I was in that cell, staying up on my bunk and staring at the ceiling. Liddle had tried to make some small talk and I just wasn't in the mood for it. I had a lot on my mind. Eventually, Liddle spoke up.

"Hey, John Lennon," he said. "Listen up. If this shit is going to work, we're going to have to talk to each other once in a while. If you don't feel like talking, that's cool, but I feel like talking. I feel like letting you know something important. You got assigned a professional mind reader. I got ESP. Show you what I mean. You're worried everybody thinks you snitched now, because you didn't go to the hole, right?"

I put down the book I was reading, climbed down from my bunk, stood right in front of him and looked him straight in the eye. It was a relief to look someone in the eye and have them make actual eye contact back at me. I hadn't expected that.

"How the hell did you know that?" I asked.

"Like I told you, I got ESP. Well, either that or above-average skills for decoding the obvious. Listen: you ain't got nothing to worry about, man."

"No?"

"No."

"Why not?"

"Because the whole damn cell block knows Kyle Freedy is J-Cat."[32]

"Yeah?"

"Yeah. They know the warden's just covering his ass by not sending you to the hole. Probably doesn't want your folks getting any more pissed off about what happened. Nobody thinks you ratted anybody out. They all know you shouldn't have been in that cell in the first place. Not only that, word got around quickly about how you handled yourself. As of yesterday, everybody on the whole goddamned block thinks you're someone who's not to be fucked with. I know *I'm* not going to fuck with you."

He smiled a little smile. It was the smile of a veteran inmate who knew the difference between a kid who was scared shitless and someone who wanted to shank him.

"You wouldn't bullshit me, would you Liddle?"

He shook his head. "Not my style."

I took a deep breath and let it out. "Thanks, man."

"No problem."

I climbed back up into my bunk and closed my eyes. I'd be lying to you if I told you I relaxed. If you ever get to Folsom, and I hope to fuck you never do, you'll find out it's not someplace anybody gets to relax. But for the first time in a long time, I slept for 11 hours straight, which counted for something. I guess I was overdrawn at the bank.

To my amazement, absolutely nobody fucked with me after I got out of solitary—verbally, physically or in any other way. Not the inmates, not the guards, nobody. They all acted like John Lennon was a powder keg that might explode at any minute.

Which was true enough as far as it went, I guess, but the powder-keg thing didn't exactly tell the whole story. The more accurate version—the version that didn't fit into a single sentence you could pass along in a couple of seconds to someone else in the yard or in the cafeteria—sounded like this: John Lennon got lucky, because even though he was scared shitless, he'd managed to get the jump on a blind guy who was about to kick his ass and maybe kill him.

John Lennon got lucky because there happened to be a tape recorder within easy reach that doubled as a lethal weapon. John Lennon got lucky because his first and second swings happened to knock the other guy out cold.

If John Lennon hadn't gotten lucky—if he'd hesitated for a few more seconds, missed one of those first swings or the blind guy had ducked and the guards had been off somewhere taking a coffee break, ignoring their job (something they did pretty regularly)—John Lennon would have been a stain on the floor of his cell by the time the guards showed up.

But none of that happened.

On my second day in my new cell, I was in the top bunk when I heard Liddle Pepper from the bunk below: "You play your cards right, you won't have any trouble from anybody here."

That sounded interesting.

"Yeah? How do you mean?"

"Think about it. What people *say* around here matters a lot more than what they see, because nobody sees everything here. Am I right?"

"Yeah. So?"

"So, all you've got to do now is *act* like you're willing to bust someone across the nose with a tape recorder, and you'll never have to do it again. People respect you. Keep giving them a reason not to *disrespect* you, and you'll be fine."

It made a lot of sense.

"You know what? You're all right, Liddle."

After a while, he said:

"And listen, I don't mean to get in your business, but if you want, I could help you out."

"How's that?"

"I could tell people you scared the shit out of me from the minute you walked in here. Tell them you're just as J-Cat as the guy you sent to the infirmary. You're not—I know that—but *they* don't know that. And life will be a hell of a lot easier for you if people *think* you are."

I had gone from the world's worst celly to the world's best. Someone at Folsom was looking out for me, and not even the deepest recesses of my natural (and acquired) paranoia could obscure that from me. This guy had absolutely nothing to gain by messing with me. He was at the very bottom of the Folsom pecking order, and he was a Level Two, like me. But he was—and this was the key point—alive. And he'd *been* alive in this snake pit for years. He had learned how to survive here.

"That would be great, Liddle," I said. "Thank you. I owe you one."

"No problem. Let me ask you a question, though."

"What's that?"

"I've been here a while. Something I've noticed: The guys who don't get fucked up here, the guys who survive, are the guys who have a plan. They want something. Could be big, could be small, but they want it. They know what it is and they work toward it, whatever it is, every day. They don't just drift along. They navigate."

I thought about this for a moment, then said: "Yeah, I guess that makes sense."

"So, what's your plan, John Lennon? What are you working towards? What do you want?"

It was a good question. I had to think about it for a minute. Finally, I said:

"You know what, man? That's something I never really gave a whole lot of thought to. Outside or inside."

"Yeah? Why not?"

"I don't know. There was always too much shit going on. Something insane I had to deal with. Something I needed to run away from. I never gave myself time to think about much else."

A long silence settled in, and I thought the conversation was over. But after a couple of minutes he said, "Yeah, but I've been here a while."

"Okay."

"And I'm telling you, John Lennon."

Big silence.

"Telling me what?" I asked.

"Guys without a plan are the ones who get fucked up. I'm just saying. I've seen it."

"Okay."

"You get it?"

"Yeah. I get it."

"So, what do you want? What's your plan?"

He wasn't letting me wiggle out of it, so I figured I might as well figure out what I wanted most in the whole world—which was actually, as it turned out, pretty obvious once I asked myself what it was.

"You know what my plan is, Liddle?"

"What's that?"

"My plan is to get the fuck out of prison and never, ever go back. Whatever it takes. I'll do that. I know a lot of guys bounce in and out, but I'm not doing that. I'm getting out of here and I'm not ever walking back in. That's the plan."

There was a little pause. Then he said: "That's a great plan, John Lennon. It's not easy. But I get the feeling you're the kind of guy who doesn't give much of a shit about easy."

"Yeah, you got that right."

"Okay, so that's a promise? You're getting out of here? And you're never coming back?"

"Yeah," I said. "That's a promise."

The lights on the cell block went out, which meant it was 11 o'clock—technically, time to stop talking. But in a low voice, I said, "Hey, Liddle."

"Yeah?"

"What's your plan?"

He sniffed. "You really want to know?"

"Yeah. I do."

"My plan is getting kids like you to realize that the plan you just came up with is the only plan. That's what *I'm* here for."

Maybe five minutes later, he started snoring. That motherfucker snored like a buzzsaw.

19. THIS AGAIN

Liddle got the word out to everyone on the cell block that I was a lunatic who was damn near impossible to control, and I started practicing my don't-fuck-with-me stare he taught me. Finally, people stopped looking at me like a piece of meat they could devour if they felt like it. Literally nobody was doing that to me anymore. I started sleeping four, maybe five consecutive hours without waking up in a cold sweat. Like I said, I didn't quite *relax*, because that wasn't really what happened at Folsom. But I felt like I could breathe again.

One night, Liddle spoke up from the bottom bunk again.

"I heard about this interesting way to get on the good side of the guards without anybody thinking you're a snitch," he said.

"Yeah? What's that?"

"You ever heard of AA?"

This again.

I laughed. Then, I started to tell him my history and about CRASH. I tell him everything, even the asshole of a teacher who abused me when I was a little kid. Liddle listens to it all, seeming to understand that it's a big thing for me to talk about all of it, and he doesn't interrupt. He lets me talk for maybe 20 minutes, and after I'm all talked out, I wrap up with, "Anyway, yeah—AA, Narcotics Anonymous, recovery? Been there, done that."

A couple minutes go by. I think the conversation is over, but it turns out it isn't.

"Yeah, absolutely, I hear you," Liddle said. "Only thing is, it's something the guards like to see. It's like—there's not really much you can do to get on the good side of the guards that doesn't get you on the bad side of somebody else, and this is one of those things. Well, two of those things."

His words hung in the air for a little while until finally, I worked up the balls to come out and say what was on my mind.

"Man, I'm not a church guy—I'm just not. And like I told you, AA? That shit did not work. Not for me, anyway. So that's just not happening"

I continued my deep dive into Frank Miller's *The Dark Knight Returns*, and after a couple more minutes went by, I noticed something: the linked ideas of light, energy and electricity were kind of like a visual playground for Miller, a playground he kept coming back to. Energy was an idea that kept popping up in his panels and kept getting connected to the various storylines.

Sometimes, the energy was channeled in constructive ways (lighting up a video arcade), and sometimes it wasn't (triggering a nuclear explosion). And it wasn't always easy to tell which kind of outcome was about to be set off.

Then, from underneath my bunk, came Liddle's voice:

"Yeah, absolutely, I hear you. Only thing is…"

Then, silence. I marked my page and put the book down.

"The only thing is what?" I asked.

"Well," Liddle explained calmly, without a hint of antagonism or any apparent desire to win or even take part in an argument. "It's just that… it's a place to go. Both of them. Church and AA. That's all I'm saying. Sometimes it's good to have a place to go, you know what I mean? And I know they're not right for you. If you think about it, though, it might be interesting to find out which one sucks *more*, from your perspective: prison church or prison meetings. In your own personal experience, I mean. That way, you'd know for sure which one to avoid, and which one sucks *least*—for you—when you need a place to go. That's the only thing."

I let myself process that for a few minutes, running it through my head a couple of times until I could finally think of something to say.

"Liddle," I said, "is this like something *you* do? Church? AA?"

"Oh, yeah," he said, without a second's hesitation. "I do both of 'em, regularly. That's why I never get any shit from the guards."

It was true. I had never seen him get so much as a dirty look from any of the guards, not even once.

"Yeah, but I'm not into being *recruited* for anything, Liddle."

"Oh, no. Of course not."

"I mean the thing is, I didn't go to church on the outside—there's a *reason* for that. And then I stopped going to meetings on the outside—there's a *reason* for that, too."

"No, no, I know that."

"Th reason was—both times, I mean—I decided I didn't want to *go*."

"Of course. No, I do get that. You've got to do you."

I started thinking about the psycho guard I ran into on day one. Not even *that* guy gave Liddle any shit—so he was right about *that* aspect, anyway.

I picked up my book again, but the second I did, I heard that voice again.

"Absolutely, I hear you. Only thing is…"

I closed the book and put it back down where it was.

"The only thing is what?"

"Prison church, prison meetings? *Way* different from church and meetings on the outside, in my experience. That's all I'm saying."

20. JESUS ISN'T DOING IT FOR ME

Finally, I went to fucking church with Liddle, though I want to be very clear about something here.

Liddle never tried to convert me. He never tried to get me to adopt any particular way of thinking about God, or recovery, or anything else, and I really respected him for that. He just wanted me to have access to a support network of some kind, and he wanted to be sure I had at least given each thing that had worked for him—church and AA—a fair shot. Once he was clear that I was willing to do that, he backed off. No more hints, no more changing the subject away from what I wanted to talk about (which was usually nothing), no more "the thing is."

He just wanted to be sure I knew people were there for me.

As I predicted it would, church bored the shit out of me, just like church on the outside had. A guy talked and read from the Bible and people prayed (or pretended to—I couldn't tell the difference, never could). Nothing sank in, and I could tell something was supposed to sink in. It was clear that church made a difference for the guys like Liddle who kept coming back to it, but it just didn't do it for me.

That night, up on the top bunk, I brought the subject up first.

"Listen, Liddle, I'm going to the AA meeting with you tomorrow, and I do appreciate you looking out for me, but I need you to know: Jesus isn't doing it for me. I'm sure he's a great guy, and I'm glad he's making a difference for you, but he's, uh, not in my plan."

"That's cool," Liddle said from below, not missing a beat. And then instantly: "Remind me what your plan is again?"

I ran my hands through my hair as I thought about what I ought to say to this before noticing that something hurt. I touched the place where it hurt again and felt a decent-sized cut on the back of my head that had only just started to heal. I hadn't seen it and nobody else had either. My hair had covered it up. It was an inch-long gash. For a second, I had no goddamned idea where it had come from. Then, I figured it out: I must have clocked myself with my own tape player in the fight with that bastard Kyle Freedy about whether I wanted him engaging in written correspondence with my mother.

With those wide swings I was taking, I had not even noticed. You're in bad shape when you don't notice delivering a blow to your own goddamned head.

That's what Folsom had done to me: made me so crazy that in a moment of rage, I had obliviously hammered my own goddamned skull.[33]

"If I survive this place," I said, "if I manage to get out of here alive, I am not coming back here, Liddle. That's my plan. And listen: my whole life up to now has been complete chaos. Just a goddamned trainwreck, I know that. I've spent a lot of time and a lot of energy being pissed off about that. But right now, I don't care whose fault that trainwreck is. I just want to get the hell out of here and not come back. I'll do whatever I have to do to make sure that happens, as long as it feels like me doing it."

He didn't say anything. He just sort of sniffed, which was kind of saying something.

The next morning, we went to a meeting together. And my whole fucking world changed.

21. A BUNCH OF GUYS IN A ROOM

In every other meeting I'd been in, when I'd said, "My name is Gary, and I'm an addict," it had been kind of like a school assignment—something that whoever was running the meeting was *making* me say.

This time, when everyone else in the circle had introduced themselves and it was my turn to say who I was, for some weird reason, it felt like the truth. A *shared* truth. Something the people in the room, including me, needed to hear.

It was just a bunch of guys in a room. Talking. Telling stories. Saying stuff like "This too shall pass," and I could tell some of them were taking it more seriously than others. But the thing that made whatever Liddle had been getting out of this suddenly matter to me, the thing that made whatever we were talking about stick, the thing that had never quite registered for me at CRASH or any other place where there had been meetings for me to go to, was: these guys were *counting on each other like it was life or death.*

Which was exactly what it was, every day, at Folsom: life or death. If you made the wrong decision or someone made the wrong decision for you, you might just end up dead. And that gave the meeting a whole new level of impact. If this didn't work, there was nothing for any of us to count on. Knowing that made the meeting way different than church, way different than any other meeting I had ever been in and a thousand times more interesting. This *had* to work. We *had* to count on each other. There was no other option if we wanted to survive and if we wanted to get clean. And I *had* to get clean.

Suddenly, "this too shall pass" was meaning a hell of a lot more to me in Folsom than it ever had on the outside. It meant there was a reason to keep doing this, to keep telling the truth. To keep listening to other people tell the truth and to keep coming back.

It dawned on me, as I sat there with Liddle, that this was a *room full of addicts.* Somehow, that had never occurred to me before. Nobody else was making us do this. It was a *room full of addicts* doing this because they had no other choice. A room full of guys with no one else to count on but the other people in the room, and nothing to rely on but a mutual agreement to share.

From one perspective, it was a bunch of guys sitting in a room for an hour and a half. But from another, it was one big share that was keeping those guys alive, an agreement to share experience, strength and hope until the next meeting.

Before that meeting, it was like there was no hope in my life, and I don't just mean my life at Folsom but every goddamned day I could remember. I literally could not remember having hope about anything.

I didn't know what it meant to keep a promise. I didn't know what it meant to get up and go to work. I didn't know what it was like to care for somebody else. I didn't know what any of that fucking meant.

As I listened to the other voices, it hit me: I was an addict. Just like everyone else in the room. It was no longer something I could ignore. I was an addict, and I had been an addict for a while. I was only barely hanging on at school until I couldn't anymore. Then, I was out on my own. Then, I was looking at my mom sobbing in the courtroom when I was being sentenced. This was addict stuff. This was what an addict's life looked like—what it sounded like and felt like. It was what I was.

Being responsible, showing up on time to places, keeping my word and things like that? Those concepts were alien to me, because I had been living without hope for so long. I was an addict, and addicts forget how to be human. Maybe I'd had some kind of idea how to be human at some point, but it was long gone now.

I was going to human school, just to learn how to exist. I was starting on the long, slow process of learning what it felt like to have hope. That meeting was where I started working on getting back to being human.

Going to meetings became the main focus of my time in Folsom. Going to meetings became part of my routine. Going to meetings became what I was all about.

Liddle was right: it *did* help to have other people to talk to and to listen to. It *did* help to have a support network. It *did* help to have a place where I belonged, a place where I knew nobody was judging me. I'd experienced that feeling of belonging before, but only for a few minutes at a time. This time around, for whatever reason—having desperation on my side, reinforcement through repetition from doing enough meetings or a combination of the two—the feeling of "this helps, and I belong here" wasn't a fleeting thing. It stuck with me.

If you counted all my time in halfway houses and at CRASH, I'd been to dozens, probably hundreds, of AA meetings. But in maximum security, for the first time in my life, all the stuff I'd heard people say in meetings was starting to click. It was starting to make a difference for me, beginning to matter enough to help me to put being in prison in context. There was one phrase in particular that kept coming up and would echo in my head, keeping me closer to sane and balanced even when I wasn't in meetings: *this too shall pass.*

That's a four-word sentence you could spend a lifetime unpacking. I'll try to do it justice here, in terms of what it meant to a 22-year-old guy navigating Folsom, holding on to recovery with white knuckles. *This too shall pass* meant that all of us addicts in the room, every single one of us, would get stronger with time as long as we stuck to the program. If we did that, then no obstacle, no amount of adversity or trash in our heads, would last forever. And PS: The trash in our heads was the real problem, not anything on the outside.

We had to accept that we were going to have ups and downs. We had to accept that our self-talk wasn't always going to support us. And we had to commit to recovery anyway.

As we dealt with the fallout from the bad choices we'd made and the lives we'd fucked up—including, but not limited, to our own—as we racked up more time being sober, we would get a little bit better, every day, at surviving. We would outlast the obstacle, whatever it was. And if we kept coming to meetings, kept sharing, kept getting and giving support, we would get better and better at staying sober, which meant getting better and better at outlasting and outgrowing our own bullshit. We would build up a resilience we could tap into when it was time to push through whatever obstacle showed up next (which, at the end of the day, would probably be some kind of head trash that we ourselves had created).

It was a great principle, a world-changing principle—but there's a catch. To get that kind of resilience and to strengthen it over time, *you had to keep coming to meetings.* It was another key piece of recovery messaging, which ended up working for me as a flipside of the first one: *Keep coming back.*

I'd never had a mantra or anything like one before, but once I started taking meetings seriously at Folsom, those two sentences became like mantras for me. I said them silently, and I said them right out loud. I said them the whole lot, day in and day out, night after night. I was pretty lucky that I had a celly who didn't much mind me talking to myself and even encouraged me when he could tell it was helping me.

And the amazing thing was that the mantras always said something back. *This too shall pass* said:

> *You're going to have good days and bad days, Gary. You're not always going to be inspired, and even the pride you feel when you're having a good day is going to turn out to be an obstacle for you to overcome. That's no problem. You're going to figure out how to get around it. Want to know why? Because you are in a marathon, not a sprint. That means you're going to get better and better over time at noticing things like obsession, self-pity and delusional thinking. These are the actual obstacles you face, not something someone else says or does. Not some event you have no control over. The actual obstacles are ultimately internal, and they are indeed under your control. In time, with*

patience, perseverance and support, you're going to figure out how to overcome them. And not only that: you're going to support and help other people as they learn to overcome those obstacles as well.

Keep coming back said:

Good news, Gary: You don't have to spend any portion of your life feeling confused, or misled, or hopelessly off track ever again—because the moment you notice one of those states of mind setting in, you now know exactly what to do next. *What you do next is work the program, which starts with getting your ass to a meeting as soon as possible. That's where the connection is. That's where the sense of belonging is. That's where the possibility of serving others and being served is. That's where the answer and the right way forward is, always—meaning every single time. Meaning* right now.

Therefore, your next step is to keep showing up. Show up for what you know is right for your recovery. What's the best way to do that? Go to a meeting today. All you have to do is show up. And the very best time to show up is right now. *So keep reaching out. Someone you know is ready to pick you up off the ground and make sure you show up in person for your own recovery at the next meeting—no matter how new you are to this, no matter what bridges you've burned and no matter how many times you think you've fucked up. One of those people is ready to make sure you get the support you need to make the right choices, starting right now. Reach out to one of them. If you do that, you'll be able to cut through the bullshit and point yourself toward the truth—your truth, not anyone else's. That's the only way forward, and going to a meeting is the best way to make sure you're headed in that direction: forward. And P.S., Gary: If you ever hear yourself muttering that you don't need meetings anymore, notice that muttering for what it is: bullshit. That noticing is a gift from your Higher Power that it's time to get your ass over to a meeting.*

Those two mantras led me into a lot of good discussions with myself. They gave me something I couldn't remember imagining I'd ever have: a daily-increasing supply of hope.

22. STICK WITH THE WINNERS

Full disclosure: I'm going to be pretty ruthless about compressing timelines from here on out. Why? Because the two lessons I picked up during the phase of my life when I finally started taking meetings seriously—*this too shall pass* and *keep coming back*—ended up being right in the fucking middle of *everything* important that happened later on, even though I found ways to pretend they didn't exist.

That means those two lessons are what really matter in what's left of this story, and they're what I'm going to be spotlighting. So, be prepared for me to hit the fast-forward button whenever something doesn't connect to those lessons.

Let me explain why I'm doing this: the thing about recovery is that it's something you accept as a lifelong process. It's not a fad or a phase or something you check off a list and consider complete. You're not "cured." You haven't "recovered." You're *in* recovery. You're part of something that you accept, right out loud, is going to take you the rest of your life to do. This is an incredibly important point. Here's how it shows up in AA's Big Book:[34]

> **"We are not cured of alcoholism [or any other addiction]. What we really have is a daily reprieve contingent on the maintenance of our spiritual condition."**

The key word there is *reprieve*. As people who are in recovery, we consider ourselves as having caught a break and having resolved to make the most of it. We accept that if we ever abuse that reprieve, if we ever *stop* working the program, we're choosing to head down a path that leads to the destruction of our most important relationships, jail, prison or even death. So, we remember that what we've actually got is a Get Out of Jail Free card that's good for 24 hours at a time, and we take recovery *one day at a time* (which is another big mantra, by the way.)

Every single day and every single second counted. No matter how long we'd been working on ourselves, our job was to do what it took *now* to stay on the right path for the next 24 hours. Nothing more, nothing less. Even people who've been clean for decades will tell you, "All that matters is today." That's all that *ever* matters.

I'd like to be able to tell you that after I got out of Folsom, I knew all of this in my bones the same way I *thought* I did while I was inside when I got serious about recovery for the first time. But this is a book about leaving the bullshit behind.

Here's the truth: What I'm going to be focusing on from here on out is the process by which I relapsed, because relapsing is something that happens. Relapsing sucks. I wouldn't wish it on my worst enemy—and I'm betting, in the pages that follow, that the clearer you get about how it happened to me, the less likely it is that relapse is going to happen to you.

***

After I had spent a little more than a year in the hellhole the residents lovingly called Old Folsom, the announcement came down from on high: a bunch of Level Twos would be moving to a nearby minimum security facility that everyone called New Folsom.

It's tempting to think that decision had something to do with my little run-in with Kyle Freedy, or with my parents putting pressure on the administrators to explain how I had landed up with a celly like him, but I don't really think one guy mattered all that much to these people. I think they just ran out of room in the old place, maybe got some heat from a politician or two who had actually read the user's manual on how to run a fucking prison, and then decided it was simpler to make this move and act like it had been their idea all along.

Regardless of *why* it was happening, I was on my way out of Old Folsom—but for some reason, Liddle, who was also a Level Two, wasn't.

I didn't have much time to say goodbye to him. We had only found out about it the day before the move was supposed to happen, and I was supposed to be ready to go the next morning. It surprised both me and Liddle when things got awkward, when we both realized how fast it was all happening. We spent the entire day trying not to talk about anything. I packed everything up in my duffel bag as instructed, I read *Cujo* and I stayed on the top bunk.

Right after lights out, I heard him from the bunk below me.

"Stick with the winners, John Lennon. And keep coming back."

"I will, man, I will—you too." My voice had cracked a little on the word "I"—twice. I pretended it hadn't happened, and he did too. I went to sleep.

The next morning, at about six and before breakfast, the guard came by and told me it was time to move. Liddle pretended he was asleep for the handoff, and I pretended I hadn't seen him open his eyes. After the guard locked the cell door behind me, I wished I'd had the balls to say thank you.

23. MASTERING THE ART OF HITTING PLAY

I was out of the war zone that was Old Folsom, but once you've spent a year in a war zone, there are after-effects. And those were what I found myself dealing with: the after-effects.

Don't get me wrong—in minimum security, the rules, both written and unwritten, that you had to live by were a lot less intense. Example: the racial stuff. As a white guy, one of the rules you had to follow in Old Folsom was: never eat food that had been eaten by a Black guy. More than that, white guys weren't supposed to socialize with Black guys *at all*. It wasn't anything the guards enforced, it was just "the way things work around here."

At Old Folsom and in county jail, older inmates warned me about this kind of thing. If you were in the cafeteria and a Black guy who was sitting at the next table happened to offer you a piece of brownie or something he hadn't finished, you couldn't accept it. You weren't even supposed to be talking to him. I thought it was stupid, but I went along with it, because I had to. But in minimum security, it was no big deal to accept that brownie, no big deal to play dominoes or talk to a Black guy.

In minimum security, I didn't really have any reason to avoid the gym, either; it was easier to be friends with people. There were a lot more options open to you in minimum security. For instance, if you wanted to, you could get a job within the prison, earn money and it would go straight into your account.

I had no problems with my celly. He was quiet, he kept to himself and he never gave me any grief. He talked to himself in the mirror sometimes, but that was no big deal. I had a lot less to worry about than I'd had in Old

Folsom—but I still felt incredibly anxious whenever I wasn't in a meeting. The anxiety went hand-in-hand with massive headaches and a piercing pain at the base of my neck. Those were there whether I was in a meeting or not.

Usually that kind of thing got better with time: we get over it, or the body heals. But for some reason, the anxiety and the physical pain just refused to get any better—actually, it was getting worse. I'd thought if the pain went away, the anxiety would go away, too, so I took Tylenol and aspirin for the pain. But nothing seemed to make any difference.

If I'd known then what I know now, I'd have realized that I was dealing with a very real problem called Complex Post-Traumatic Stress Syndrome (C-PTSD)—but I didn't know that. Even if I had, there wasn't a therapist within a light-year of the facilities connected to the one I was locked up in who would've been able to treat it.

I listened to a lot of Suicidal Tendencies. *That* was my therapy—hitting the play button. Let me tell you, I mastered the art of hitting play. The music helped me get through the day, but it didn't make the after-effects of Old Folsom any easier to deal with. When the music stopped, they were always there.

***

I thought that shifting over to a less dangerous place in the penal system would help me feel better, physically and mentally. Instead, exactly the opposite happened. The reason for that, I have since figured out, is that human beings just aren't made for places like Old Folsom.

Our brains know, on some weirdly deep level, that we're not supposed to be in environments like that—but sometimes we end up there anyway. To protect us, our brains come up with whatever coping mechanisms necessary to enable us to survive, and sometimes, that means messing with our mind in bizarre ways. *Hey,* the brain says, *it's better than fucking dying, right?*

Thank you, brain, yes—it definitely is better than dying. But it's also no way to live.

When I finally got moved to minimum security, my brain did anything and everything it could think of to make sure I compartmentalized all the crap I had ever gone through in my life, including all the insane shit I'd gone through at Old Folsom. My brain kept it buried deep down inside so it couldn't possibly get out. My brain had figured out, very quickly, that showing weakness could get me killed. My brain was, to be fair, only doing its job—never mind that rumbling underfoot.

Burying stuff equals survival—it always has, right? it said.[35]

What could possibly go wrong?

PART THREE: THE FELLOWSHIP OF THE RING

In Part Three, I make it out of Folsom and start trying to make sense of life on the outside. I get a sponsor and set up a support network. I get a job. I get married to someone I was in recovery with, which turns out not to be a great idea. I work some stuff out with my dad, then lose him. I reconnect with Melissa, my old girlfriend from high school. And as always, I fixate on pop culture.

To fast-forward over the last year or so of my time in Folsom Prison: I got a job filing and ordering for Folsom's procurement department, ordering prescription drugs for the inmates. Which I guess, technically, means I was still a drug dealer.

Up until then, just about all my jobs on the outside had been retail, and I hadn't given a shit about them. This one, though, I knew I had to hold on to. If I wanted to be released, I had to be a model prisoner. That meant showing up on time, doing what was expected, keeping the boss happy and staying out of trouble—all of which I did.

Somehow, though, at the exact same time I was making sure I didn't fuck up on this job, I went completely insane.

For months on end, I withdrew. I stopped talking to people, with the only exceptions of meetings and short discussions with my boss. I built my own little routine and my own little world, and I lost myself in it (think Robert De Niro in *Taxi Driver*). I exercised relentlessly, went to work, filed stuff, came back to my cell and got ready to do it all again.

I wrote a lot, because people at my meetings were always saying journaling would help me. All I was really doing with my "journaling," though, was freaking out about how little time there was to get ready for life on the outside. Eventually, I just started listing stuff. The more time I spent making lists, the less time I had to think about the problem of how I would cope on the outside, which scared the shit out of me.

I started writing about what time I woke up, what I ate, what time I left for work, when I took a shit, what time I went to sleep and back to what time I woke up again. Soon, the journal was *nothing but* the dates and times of my daily activities, of everything I could think of. I filled dozens of pages with this stuff.

My mind was totally out of control.

24. OPERATION DON'T FUCK UP

For my last six months in Folsom, I was basically a volcano rumbling until the next explosion, and I knew exploding was something I had to *keep* from happening if I wanted to get out of prison and stay out. So, I had a strategy for not fucking up, one that seemed to work. Don't ask me why it worked—it just did.

My strategy was: make lots of lists, lists of whatever I had just done:

Wake up.
Exercise while listening to music.
Write down what I just did.
Go to work.
Come back.
Write down what I just did.
Go to a meeting.
Write down what I just did.
Exercise while listening to music.
Eat.
Come back to the cell.
Write down what I just did.
Exercise while listening to music.
Write down what I just did.
Go to bed.
Fall asleep.
Repeat.

I felt more in control when I did that, and the ground seemed to rumble a little less beneath my feet. I was doing it all to avoid having to think about the question that scared the living shit out of me: *What the hell is going to happen to me when I get out of here?*

I had no marketable skills and no support network other than my parents, and God only knew how many bridges I had burned with them. I had no plan. I had nothing.

If the volcano blew again, I'd start using again. If I started using again, I'd get busted again. If I got busted again, I'd end up back in Folsom, and not for just a couple of years—for good. How the fuck was I going to keep that from happening? What was the *plan?*

I kept not having any good answer to that question, so I focused on a question I thought I *could* answer: *How can I get through the next nine months without fucking up and extending my sentence?*

The answer that came back, over and over, was to do stuff that seemed healthy and then write down what I did:

Wake up.
Exercise while listening to music.
Write down what I just did.
Go to work. Come back.
Write down what I just did.
Go to a meeting.
Write down what I just did.
Exercise while listening to music.
Eat.
Come back to the cell.
Write down what I just did.
Exercise while listening to music.
Write down what I just did.
Go to bed.
Fall asleep.
Repeat.

It was what I now call Operation Don't Fuck Up. I fell into a relentless routine of compartmentalizing everything I was going through by compulsively focusing on the ritual of writing lists of my activities. And that compartmentalization poisoned me in mind, body and spirit.

I got sick and lost a ton of weight, and I ended up going to the infirmary; they said it was some kind of viral infection, but who knows. They gave me antibiotics to take, and I took them, but the pills didn't make any difference. I got even sicker and lost even more weight. The pain at the back of my neck and the headaches got even worse. What the fuck was happening to me?

Wake up.
Exercise while listening to music.
Write down what I just did.
Go to work.
Come back.
Write down what I just did.
Go to a meeting.
Write down what I just did.
Exercise while listening to music.
Eat.
Come back to the cell.
Write down what I just did.
Exercise while listening to music.
Write down what I just did.
Go to bed.
Fall asleep.
Repeat.

I had come into prison at 210 pounds and was now down to 140 pounds. I had lost 70 pounds over a period of about six months—no shit. As I was nearing the finish line of doing my time at Folsom, I looked like someone who had been in a fucking concentration camp.

I kept having to go back to the doctor at the infirmary, who ordered me to take it easy. It meant that I stopped going to work, which didn't help with the weight loss. The doctor also made me stop exercising so goddamn much, worrying about ways I might put on weight.

Wake up.
Listen to music.
Write down what I just did.
Go to the infirmary.
Come back.
Write down what I just did.
Go to a meeting.
Write down what I just did.
Lie down while listening to music.
Eat.
Come back to the cell.
Write down what I just did.
Lie down while listening to music.
Write down what I just did.
Go to bed.
Fall asleep.
Repeat.

In the end, that fixation on my routine did work in one way: time had passed, and I hadn't fucked up. I hadn't gotten in trouble, and I hadn't had my sentence extended.

I was a deeply, deeply messed up person who looked like I had been through a war, because I had. But one morning, Intense Eyes—the guard who had handed me the scissors back on day one—showed up, unlocked my cell and told me I'd completed my sentence. There was the tiniest hint of a smile in his eyes, which were usually so cutting and hard that they made you feel like you were about to regret eyeballing him. It was like he was telling me I hadn't let him down after all.

I stepped out of the cell and followed him. I was going home, wherever that was.

25. RE-ENTRY

The most amazing fucking thing happened.

After all that paranoia, all that insanity, all that physical and mental shuddering—which, looking back, felt a little like I was aboard the Apollo 13 as it re-entered Earth's atmosphere, hoping its heat shields would hold—my actual, immediate re-entry into the world I had left behind was seamless, painless and disaster-free.

It all unfolded in a bizarrely positive cloud of total, bulletproof good feelings. That cloud of bulletproof positivity stayed with me for about two weeks. It was the last thing I expected, but it happened.

Inside prison, for the last eight months or so of my sentence, there had been these relentless oncoming tidal waves of shit—a tsunami of shit I couldn't stop worrying about, wave after never-ending wave of shit I had gone through and was afraid to go through, bulging, accelerating waves headed straight for me that made me sick inside every time I saw them on the horizon. Inside, the waves seemed to get bigger, more powerful and closer every day. But the day I walked out, that oncoming tsunami somehow vanished. It collapsed into the sea without touching a thing on the shore.

That first day was glorious. My mom and dad came to pick me up, all smiles and no judgment, without even a syllable of negativity uttered. They were just glad to have me back and alive, and I was glad to be back and alive. All of us agreed on that, and that was the starting point.

We got in their car and my dad drove us to Denny's while I sat in the back like a celebrity or something. In the booth, I scanned the menu before ordering a Grand Slam: two pancakes, two eggs over easy, two bacon strips and two sausage links. For some reason, the act of sitting in a restaurant with the rest of the world, being able to order whatever the hell I wanted from the menu and then have it show up, blew my fucking mind. I'll never forget it. I'd never had a meal like that and I never will again. It was one of the most beautiful experiences of my entire life.

The sheer, massive gratitude of free will and free action got me high. This was a high that made all other highs I had ever experienced suddenly seem tiny, irrelevant, beside the point. I had never even thought about the possibility of getting high like that in a Denny's, without drugs and with my parents sitting across the table from me. But that's what happened.

Living in the moment was making me so grateful that I wanted to cry. I am pretty sure I did cry over that fucking Grand Slam.

I had gotten crazy and old before my time in Folsom, but I had made it out—and I never had to go back, ever again, as long as I stayed clean. It was something I could choose to do if I wanted to, and man, did I want to.

I didn't need anything. I wasn't going to get hung up on that incoming tidal wave of shit or on what might happen in the future, be it right or wrong, good or bad. The tidal wave was gone now, and for the moment, I was simply grateful. I could order a Grand Slam and eat it if I wanted to. I could, Jesus, go to the beach—get my feet wet in the ocean again. If I wanted to.

My folks mentioned that my bicycle was still in the garage where I had left it. That meant I could ride my bike if I wanted to—or not. I could go for a walk if I wanted to. It was up to me. I was driving my own fucking life again.

After everything I had been through, that day was unbelievable, but I kept right on believing in it, and it felt better every time I did.

26. CLOUD NINE, ENCINITAS AND BALLSACK

I call the couple of weeks that followed that Grand Slam my Cloud Nine period. Everything, and I do mean everything, was good.

I felt inner peace for the first time in my life. I was perfectly happy, morning, noon and night, no matter what happened. It didn't last, mind you, but it did happen, and I did know at the time what a big deal that was.

I had never felt that kind of peace before. The anxiety was gone. The pride was gone. The need to get back at teachers, society, at anybody else who felt like telling me I was a loser, was gone. Suddenly, all of that bullshit was gone—all the nightmares and all the trauma. Apparently, none of it mattered anymore. Prison had stripped me of all my pride.[36]

The sheer, overwhelming gratitude I felt for having made it *out* of prison had stripped me of my anxieties and any need to get back at anyone. I felt great. I had no idea how long Cloud Nine would last, but I wanted it to last forever—and that desire kept me motivated to go to meetings.

Within 48 hours of getting out, I found out about and went to a meeting in Encinitas, which happens to be a very, very beautiful place—all storybook rolling hills and gorgeous beaches. The beaches were populated by epic-cool, too-stunning-for-words surfer ladies who looked like they had somehow managed to ride their boards over all the obstacles the universe had ever sent their way and would keep doing so indefinitely. They were gorgeous, and I am here to tell you, they left an impression on me. It had been quite a while since I'd been in a position to appreciate the beauty of women in person.[37]

Somehow, I had transitioned from hell (meaning prison) right into paradise. As I made my way toward the church where the meeting was scheduled to happen, I was still very much on Cloud Nine. I felt like I was catching yet another break: the setting of my very first meeting out of Folsom was having a powerful, positive impact on me. The smell of the ocean, the gentle slope of the hills, the parade of young, fit, optimistic, energetic surfer-angel-women: it all seemed like a movie set that had been built just for me. It was a scene I was meant to be cast in.

Everything seemed possible in Encinitas. It was the perfect spot to have my first meeting after escaping from gladiator school, and it was exactly what I needed.

During that first meeting, I noticed a big, rusty-looking, barrel-chested guy in the group with a beard and mustache. He looked weirdly familiar. It was Ballsack, a huge guy who could down a fifth of vodka before you asked him for the time. Back before his current beard and 'stache, in the old days, we'd done a lot of partying together.

I recognized him before he recognized me (remember: I'd lost a lot of weight and I'd been through a lot). When he finally did recognize me, this big, wild grin spread across his face. I definitely remembered that grin.

Then, another guy recognized me before I recognized *him*.

"Gary! No *way!*"

The guy who said this was pale and thin as a rail, I guess because God wanted to make sure I had a memorable contrast to Ballsack in that first meeting on the outside. He was Don Wan.

Don Wan and I had been partners in crime, literally and figuratively, for a couple of weeks back when I was dealing meth. We were both serious about getting high and about metal music back then—and that was the complete list of things we were serious about. Now, somehow, I could tell with just one glance: he was sober, and he was serious about staying that way.

Irony of ironies, one of the promises I had made myself in Folsom was to stay away from the old crowd I used to hang with when I was using *no matter what.* That was Job One, as far as I was concerned. But during that very first meeting, there were two guys I'd done meth with, two guys from the bad old days, Ballsack and Don Wan, who listened most attentively as I shared and who were there to hug me once the meeting ended.

Ballsack and Don Wan each instantly became part of my support team—that much was obvious even before the meeting ended.[38] I amended my promise to myself: Job One was to stay away from the Old Crowd... *unless* they happened to show up at a meeting.

Ballsack had been sober for three-and-a-half years, making him an elder statesman in terms of sobriety compared to me and Don (seven months). Each of them was, in calendar terms, was a little younger than me. Once the meeting broke up, the three of us stepped outside and found a place in the parking lot where we could talk, and I gave them much more detail about what had happened to me in Folsom than I'd been willing or able to share in the group.

There was a whole lot to fill them in on, so we stood outside that church and talked for maybe an hour and a half. Near the end of our conversation, Ballsack (who had finally gotten tired of me running my mouth) looked straight at me and said: "You do know what a sponsor is, right?"

I kept his gaze and nodded, although to be perfectly honest, I wasn't exactly sure what the *formal* definition was. I had probably zoned out or been in denial when it had come up in other meetings I'd been to, but I had an intuitive sense of what it was.

"It's someone you report to," I said, "like a parole officer for AA."

Don gave a little chuckle. Ballsack ignored this, maintaining calm eye contact with me and shaking his head slowly.

"Your sponsor is not your parole officer," he said. "Not your therapist, either. Not your mom. Not your dad. Your sponsor is someone who's been where you've been and who's there for you to talk to if there's something you need to say—something that, for whatever reason, you can't say during the meeting. Something that needs to be talked about for you to work the program. Got it?"

I nodded.

"Do you want me to be your sponsor?" he asked.

I nodded again.

"Listen, Gary. I bring two things to the table: experience and accountability. I can share the experience with the program that I have with you, and I'm happy to do that. But we *both* need to share the accountability. Meaning: we are here to make clear future commitments to each other. Mine is to be there for you when you need to talk, and yours is to keep coming back. Are you willing to make that commitment?"

I kept looking him in the eye, took a deep breath and decided I definitely was.

"Yes," I said. He put out his hand and I shook it.

"We're in business," said Ballsack, smiling. "Something else you ought to know, because you were in Folsom—I was in San Quentin for a year. I've got an idea what you've been through. I'm thinking that the main reason you're here talking to me right now is that you really, really don't want to go back there. I figure you should probably know that I made myself a promise when I got out: I'm *never* fucking going back there. Never. If things ever get bad again, if they ever try to send me back inside, they're not going to get the chance. I'll kick it in the head. I'm not kidding. Anyway, why do I mention this? Seems like we both want the same thing: life on the outside. So, let's do that, okay?"

Wow. That got real—real quick.

"Yeah, let's do that," I replied.

I knew exactly where Ballsack was coming from, but our exchange seemed to freak Don Wan a bit, and he was eager to change the subject.

"Now for the big question," Don said.

"What's that?"

"Have you got a job?"

27. THE WHEREHOUSE

Don Wan—recovering addict, Metallica fan and all-around great guy—got me a job, much to the relief of my parents, who didn't mind seeing evidence that I was capable, theoretically, at least, of standing on my own two feet.[39] As it happened, Don was the manager at a local music and video store called The Wherehouse, which was part of a regional chain.

This was 1993. If you happened to have been born right before, around or later than 1993, you may not have heard much about The Wherehouse. It's probably a bit like hearing someone lecture about ancient history when I tell you that this was one of retail music's dominant players on the West Coast retail back in the early '90s, a very big-deal chain.

It may feel like even more ancient-history when I mention that, in 1993, recorded entertainment was CDs and cassette tapes for music and VHS videotapes for movies. Streaming wasn't a thing. Vinyl record sales had already begun to crater when I walked into Folsom in 1991, and by the time I got out, they'd collapsed to nearly nothing and most people assumed it was basically a dead medium.

Anyway—the point is, Don Wan knew I loved music and movies, and he saw a connection between where he worked and what I loved, so he gave me a job. He also personally trained me, and I started as a clerk at The Wherehouse.

I worked part-time at the video counter, helping customers find what they were looking for, processing payments for their chosen VHS rentals (a big boxy thing some of you older people might remember) and checking their rentals back into inventory once they were done watching them. Since this was the '90s, all of it happened in person—can you imagine? Anyway, Don trained me in all of that as well as the basics of customer service.

As a chain, the Wherehouse had been renting VHS videos to people for nearly a decade, and by the time I came on, they were competing with a much larger national chain: Blockbuster. The Wherehouse would eventually go bankrupt and Blockbuster would lose the market-share race to an outfit called Netflix that you may have heard of—but all of that was far, far in a future I couldn't possibly have predicted when I came on board as a rookie, 24-a-week counter guy.

I mention all this only to give you some personal context: I was a video clerk with a love for pop culture and big, big dreams—a lot like Quentin Tarantino had been just a few years earlier. Tarantino's movie *Reservoir Dogs* had come out the previous year, and I'd heard how he'd moved, against all odds, into the Hollywood big-time—but I hadn't seen his stuff. I fantasized about making a similar kind of move, but I had zero idea how, nor what medium might help me.

I just knew I loved comic books and movies and music, and I knew I felt totally alive when I talked about them. It was the only part of the big, big dream I had in focus—though maybe it wasn't even a dream. Maybe it was just Cloud Nine doing the talking, but for the first time in my life, I felt like I was on the right track.

Sponsor? Check.

Job? Check.

Normie friends who aren't addicts? Check.

Don Wan really was a friend, by the way—he wasn't just my boss. In addition to hiring me, training me and generally keeping an eye on me at the Wherehouse, all of which constituted a major commitment—because remember, other than the filing job at Folsom, I had never felt much like holding onto a real job—he proved beyond a doubt that he was an all-around great guy one Tuesday night.

That night, he took me to see *Reservoir Dogs*, which he said I would love—and he was right. The film blew my fucking mind.

I'd never seen anything like it, because *nobody* had ever seen anything like it. It was its own genre, right out of the gate: the frank, explicit and outrageous dialogue delivered without apology. The carefully choreographed slow-motion mayhem. The opinionated, foul-mouthed characters with colors instead of real names, men who seemed ready to die on whatever conversational hill they happened to find themselves on.

As they defended non-negotiable views on sex, work, cops, torture, pop culture, you name it, they never seemed to agree. Regardless, they had planned a heist together that went sideways. Along the way, they argue about everything and nothing. Life. Death. Madonna. Comic books! It was a masterpiece, and I loved it all.

This was, for me, the cinematic promised land. Gen X had officially entered the building. So cool. So slick. So perfect. Later on, Don Wan and I went to see *True Romance*, which Tarantino wrote, and it was another instant classic. Even if a lot of people didn't realize it at the time, Don Wan and I did.

We both should have known that daily life on Cloud Nine wasn't going to last forever, but it was still a bit of a shock when my batteries gave out. I was working the video counter at the Wherehouse when it happened.

I caught sight of this old dude in a baggy sweater stalking toward the video department with death in his blue-grey eyes, his mouth set tight like he had just been forced to swallow a dose of quick-dry concrete. This guy had me in his sights, and I could tell right away that he did not like what he saw. As he approached, he was waving a VHS box around like it was a piece of evidence for the jury to remember when they sent me to the fucking electric chair. Old guys telling me off were a real threat to my newfound serenity, though I didn't know that at the time.

"Hey, you—you know what you *said* was in this box yesterday? Do you? *Well?*"

For a moment, I was so startled I couldn't say anything. I gripped the counter and pursed my lips, feeling the volcano start to rumble deep inside me.

"Well, I'll tell you," the old man continued. "You told me this box had a copy of *Batman* starring Michael Keaton in it—remember that little conversation?"

Actually, I didn't. I took a deep breath, but the rumbling in the pit of my stomach was getting louder.

"Don't tell me you don't remember it, because I know you do. Want to take a guess as to what was actually *in* this box when I got home? Let me give you a little hint. *Not* Michael Keaton, and *not Batman.* You gave me a copy of *Pretty in Pink* instead. Now, what I want to know is, what are you going to *do* about it?"

Personally—and this is the fascinating part, looking back on it— I actually believed I was behaving in a restrained and professional way when the volcano blew. I had made a conscious decision not to slug the guy, or to touch him in any shape, manner or fashion, which seemed to me the height of professionalism.

Maybe my understanding of basic customer service protocols was a bit off at that point in my career, though, because what I *did* do was *light that old bastard up* verbally, which I've since learned you aren't supposed to do to customers.

"Listen, man," I said, "if you really want to take this outside so you and I can dance, you need to know, I am *all in.* And I'm going to predict the outcome of that little discussion for you, old man, just so you can make the right decision: I would *fuck you up.* And something else to consider? I would enjoy *every goddamned minute of it.* You don't get to walk in here waving that shit around and shouting at people, you got that? Now, are you going to take a deep breath, step back and give yourself an attitude adjustment so we can talk about your fucking *Molly Ringwald video,* or do we have a *problem* here?"

I hadn't realized how loud I'd been talking, but I started thinking there might have been a *bit* of volume problem on my side when the deathly silence that had taken over the store crossed the 30 second mark, give or take.

I spotted Don Wan running from the front of the store toward the video section; he must have been manning the registers when he heard the volcano erupt. By the time he got to my counter, stepped in front of me and started apologizing profusely and breathlessly to the old guy, whose jaw was slack, I figured I might have gone a bit too far.

Later—much later, if I'm honest—it began to dawn on me that my response to the old guy's problem might have been not just a volume problem, but a content problem.

28. "THE WORLD YOU'RE IN NOW"

"Dude. I went out on a *limb* for you. You cannot *do* shit like that. What the hell were you *thinking?*"

For some reason—probably a clear memory of a time that he'd fucked up spectacularly in his own life—Don Wan didn't begin a one-on-one discussion in the back office to fire me, which he would have been completely within his rights to do (and which, if I'm honest, was kind of what I expected), but that's not what happened. Instead, he tried to salvage the situation. He was looking for a reason *not* to fire me.

"That wasn't a rhetorical question, Gary," he continued. "I'm seriously trying to figure out what was going through your head."

"Okay."

"What made you think that was acceptable? Talking to a *customer* like that? Take some time. Think about that. Then, please, please tell me what you were thinking. I need to know. *You* need to know."

"Okay."

For maybe the first time in my life, after an "authority figure" asked me what in the world I had been thinking when I'd done...*whatever*...I called a time-out. I tried to figure out what *had* caused me to go off on that old guy waving a video box in my face. Don Wan was my boss, which technically made him The Man—and the Man was someone I had never gotten along with particularly well. But he was also a friend, one who had gone out on a limb for me to give me this opportunity.

It was a fair question: What *had* I been thinking? We both deserved an answer to that question.

We sat there for what felt like forever. I stared at my shoes, but I wasn't looking at my shoes. I was replaying the whole thing, trying to figure out what had set me off. I was watching the old guy in his baggy sweater walk toward me with that look of hatred in his eyes, waving that VHS box all around. I replayed the moment over and over.

When the answer suddenly surfaced, it was like Don Wan and I were at an AA meeting. I knew I could share what had happened, what I had figured out about the situation and my reaction to it without being judged.

"I thought he was disrespecting me," I said. "He *was* disrespecting me. It was a Folsom thing. If you let somebody disrespect you in Folsom, you're that person's bitch. And that's not something you let happen."

Don Wan took that in. He nodded. He looked thoughtful and did a slow intake of oxygen through his nose as he kept nodding, like he'd understood what I just said and was choosing to do a reset of everything. For both of us. He was clearing the air between us and giving me a second chance. Not just a second chance to keep my job, but a second chance to listen.

Finally, he exhaled and said: "This is a different world, though, Gary."

"Okay."

"And the thing is: it's the world you're in now."

"Okay."

"Understood?"

"Understood."

***

From that point on, Cloud Nine was an on-and-off kind of thing, though here, I need to be very clear about something: it wasn't the old guy yelling at me about a mis-boxed video that made Cloud Nine recede.

Cloud Nine was always going to recede. This was just the first time I *felt* it receding for long enough to make a terrible choice. Cloud Nine would come back again, but it would always recede again, too. That's life. Unfortunately, it got easier and easier for me to notice that cloud of joy and gratitude dissipating in the weeks that followed.

Again: I'm not saying I stopped experiencing joy and gratitude. What I'm saying is that the early sensation I got once I made it out of Folsom, the sensation that the world finally made sense and would make sense *all the time*, the sensation that getting through the day would be fairly simple and would *stay* fairly simple as long as I kept going to meetings, vanished. But it was not because of a conversation I had with a cranky customer at the Wherehouse. It was because I was a human being who still hadn't gotten to the bottom of my own experience of multiple episodes of trauma.

In other words: the honeymoon was over.

The difficulty getting to sleep came back. The nightmares about being in prison came back, and whenever they did, I would sit bolt upright in bed—then, I'd have to spend about five minutes trying as hard as I could to persuade my own brain that I wasn't in Folsom anymore.

When someone would walk up behind me, I'd flinch and spin around, ready as hell to check the "fight" box in the instant, pop-up fight-or-flight questionnaire, embedded deep in our DNA. When it finally became clearer to me on an emotional level that I wasn't about to be murdered, I'd have to find some way to explain that to myself, which wasn't always easy.

And then there was something Don Wan had already noticed: whenever I went to a movie theatre, I had to sit in the very back row—anywhere else and I couldn't enjoy the film, and neither could anyone with me. I'd constantly be looking over my shoulder to make sure nothing was gaining on me from behind.

In the post-Cloud Nine phase, I had to accept that it wasn't all going to be perfect. Adjusting to life on the outside—hell, adjusting to life *at all*—was going to take ongoing effort on my part. Staying sober was going to take ongoing effort. Not scaring the normies was going to take ongoing effort. I decided to be cool with all that.

I kept going to meetings. I kept going to work. I kept checking in with Ballsack.

When I talk about this period of my life, the part right after Folsom, sometimes people ask me whether I ever looked for a therapist to talk to. I did—but the therapists I ended up finding were either so overwhelmed with other patients or so incompetent that they really didn't do me much good. That sounds harsh, maybe, but it's what I and a lot of other people have experienced trying to find mental health professionals who will step up, diagnose us properly and deliver the treatment we need.

Somehow, if you have a visible physical health problem, like, say, a broken leg, nobody expects you to suck it up and figure out how to solve the problem on your own. People don't say, "You know, there comes a point in life where you have to grow up. If you put your mind to it, you wouldn't have a broken leg." They take you to the emergency room.

But if you have a mental health issue that isn't obvious at first glance, the system doesn't always know what to do with you—but that's not even the worst part. The worst part is you run into a lot of people who act like you really ought to be able to heal yourself, like you just lack the necessary willpower or character or whatever else you need to make your life work. And yes, There are therapists who act like that. There shouldn't be. But there are.

I knew I *needed* therapy; that was pretty obvious. But locating the *right* therapist was not an easy thing. I'd track one down, talk to that person a couple of times, decide it wasn't working and try to find someone else, because if you can't talk to a therapist about anything, there's no fucking point. Then, I would repeat the process.

You can burn up a lot of time that way. I should also mention that really good therapists were (and still are) pretty expensive, and I didn't feel like making my parents spend any more money on this kind of thing than was absolutely necessary. Bottom line: going to meetings became my therapy. And that, as it turned out, was not all that bad of an approach. After all, the meetings *were* group therapy, and honestly, they served me pretty well.

After the "honeymoon" phase of being out of prison wore off, after it was obvious I needed to talk to *somebody* about all the crap I was going through, after I'd test-driven a bunch of the available meeting environments and found three or four that made me feel welcome and like I belonged...I realized I could talk to *these* people (not just Ballsack) about anything. As in, anything. So, I ended up sharing quite a lot about what I was doing to cope with what I could only describe at the time as "being freaked out."[40]

I shared. And shared. And shared.

Hey. I'm Gary and I'm an addict. I just got out of prison.
I don't want to go back.
I went off on this guy at work who was being an asshole, but who didn't deserve to have me go off on him.
I'm trying to adjust.
I was abused when I was a little kid.
I got in a lot of trouble when I was growing up.
I put my parents through hell.
I had a major meth habit, and I did all kinds of other drugs before I got clean.
I went to jail, then went to Folsom and started taking recovery seriously while I was inside.
I've been clean for X months, Y days, and I don't want to fuck that up. (I kept careful track of the time, like a lot of recovering addicts.)
What the hell do I do?

Sometimes, the answers that came back when I said stuff like this to the group weren't anything I hadn't heard before. But hearing them from people who had more experience navigating recovery than I had, though, was a huge boost for me, mentally and emotionally. The answers—which usually included *this too shall pass* and *keep coming back*—always helped me hang on. And every time I decided to hang on for another day, I made a point of writing down *why* I had made that decision in my latest notebook.[41]

Other times, I'd hear something brand new, something I hadn't considered before. Something that gave me a whole new perspective on my situation. At one meeting, someone quoted this sentence from the Big Book:

> **"We will not regret the past nor wish to shut the door on it."**

I wrote that down, too.

29. CUE THE HIGHLIGHT REEL

We're about to shift into highlight reel mode now. I'm going to crunch a whole lot of time into a few paragraphs for you.

I knew I wasn't going to be able to make a career out of The Wherehouse. I *did* learn how to hold down a job—you know, like grownup human beings do—while I was there though, and that was all thanks to Don Wan, a great friend and a great boss. I was grateful for his presence in my life back then, and I'm grateful for it now, but you're not going to be hearing any more about him. Like I said: highlight reel mode.

I'm grateful, too, for how much Ballsack helped me during this period. He never, ever gave up on me, even though I had to be one of the most crap sponsees in the history of the recovery movement—perpetually showing up late, forgetting about clear future commitments, dropping names left and right from meetings that I really shouldn't have been dropping (like that rock star I mentioned earlier).

Ballsack had this way of coming up with just the creative course-correction message I needed, a message that didn't make me feel like he thought I was a piece of dirt on his shoe, which was how a lot of other "authority figures" in my life had made me feel. Ballsack found a way to make me smile instead. ("Hey, remind me—why do we call it Narcotics Anonymous again? Oh, right, it's *anonymous,* I see…so, that means we *don't* tell anyone the first and last names of the people we were just in meetings with. Okay, thanks, Gary—got it.")

Anyway.

Like I said, I kept going to meetings, I kept sharing and I kept taking notes. When things got difficult, meetings were what got me through the week. Meetings were, to me, what the Fellowship of the Ring was to Frodo—I'm talking about the series of unlikely alliances designed to help Frodo Baggins get the One Ring to Mordor so he could destroy it in the flames of Mount Doom. If you know those books well, you know that the Fellowship went through a lot of changes. So did mine, as it turned out. But the fact remains: when I felt hopeless, when I freaked out or when money got tight, I knew the Fellowship was there.

And by the way, money was *always* tight.

I got a couple of jobs to supplement my hours at the Wherehouse. I got a part-time job working in a comic book store, for instance, which was a gig I really loved. My shifts there gave me brief, welcome bursts of the same kind of euphoria I'd felt on Cloud Nine, but my income was inconsistent. I could never be sure how many hours I was going to get at the store from week to week. Eventually, I got a job doing parts delivery that was, financially at least, a little more attractive. By then, I was out of my parents' place and making a go of it on my own, so that was exciting.

To keep fast-forwarding, I kept going to meetings, I met someone at one of them and I got married. Spoiler alert: that marriage didn't work out. You'll start to find out what the final months of that relationship looked like in a minute (remember, we're in highlight-reel mode here), but before I map that out, let me just say up front two things I know now that I didn't know back then.

First, if you're an addict, it's a mistake to get emotionally involved with someone you meet at a meeting. And second, it's a mistake to get married too early, and the formula of t (time) > too early has a lot more to do with your emotional age than with your chronological age.

Chronologically, I was 26, but emotionally, I was about six on a bad day—and I had a *lot* of bad days. I wasn't getting the treatment I needed, and I had a lot of unresolved issues. Communication was not my strong suit, I tended toward self-absorption and I consistently forgot all about shit that was extremely important to other people in my life. Going in, let's just say I did not have a particularly high-percentage shot at making a marriage work.

Now, here's the key point I need to land with you about my first marriage, which is a big part of what comes next. It may sound, at times, in the chapters you're about to read, like I believe I didn't make any big mistakes along the way in my first marriage. It may sound like I think the other person in this relationship—whose real name I'm not sharing here because she's a good person who doesn't deserve any more crap than life has already thrown her way—made most of the big mistakes.

She didn't.

There were a lot of times I thought she did and acted like she did, but that's the story I told myself at the time. Looking back, I can see that that narrative was bullshit. We each found plenty of things to fuck up. I had to say that clearly here.

Moving on, there's a Guns 'N Roses song called "One in a Million" where Axl Rose sings about some people saying you're lazy, other people saying that's "just you being you," and still other people saying you're crazy, leaving you guessing whether you *are* crazy after all. That's the song I'll hand you before I give you the next interesting story from Gary's Bag of Interesting Stories, the song that will have to do when it comes to summing up where I was at in the mid-Nineties.

And listen: Everything's on YouTube now, so why don't you stop right now—no, I'm not kidding, stop before you turn this fucking page—and go fire up YouTube. Listen to that song. Right now, please. I'll meet you back here once you get done checking in with Axl.

And by the way: if the lyrics piss you off, maybe consider getting over it. That's how he felt at the time. That's what he needed to go through to write a song about saying out loud to the whole world, at the top of his lungs, that he was still figuring out what was right and wrong. That he hadn't been certain about right and wrong for as long as he could remember. That he knows he's here for *some* fucking reason, and he's going to keep looking for it until he finds it. He's going to keep moving on.

That's the last part of the highlight reel: that song. It meant a lot to me. Maybe it will mean something to you.

And if you didn't stop and go to YouTube, please understand: I am not joking. Grow a pair. Go listen to that song. Then we can do business.

30. BREAKING THE UNWRITTEN RULE

I met my first wife (let's call her Shelly) in rehab. That's never a good place to go if you're looking for a life partner, no matter how straight-edge you are or plan to be. It's actually kind of an unwritten rule: don't get into a relationship early in recovery. We did it anyway.

The only thing Shelly and I *had in common* was recovery. Outside of that, it was a real effort for us to find any points of contact. For instance, Shelly wasn't anywhere near as obsessive as I was about comic books—and films, TV shows, music and pretty much any other expression of pop culture. For me, these things were not distractions from real life. They *were* real life.

Shelly didn't see it that way. For her, comic books and movies were entertainment, period. They had no real importance once they'd been experienced. They were passing events like weather, or clothes you were done with and then donated to Goodwill. She did like to read, but she didn't form the same kind of ongoing attachment to the books themselves that I did.

Also, she was a natural introvert, whereas I operate at the extreme end of extroversion. I'm not just social, I'm *aggressively* social. And usually, what I'm aggressively social *about* is movies, comic books and television shows. Given what I *now* do for a living—make YouTube videos about pop culture, specifically about nerd culture—you can probably tell that Future Gary has figured out what 1993 Gary hadn't quite realized: the relationship was not built to last.

It definitely wasn't, but the two of us not having the same level of interest in comic books and movies was not the *only* reason this marriage failed, and I can't pretend it was. Honestly, I am a difficult person to live with.

Like Peter Parker, I've got a lot of hangups. I've got ADHD, I've got OCD, I'm deeply opinionated and I have very little patience. Even if she and I hadn't disagreed about things like the cultural and personal importance of *Spider-Man*, I'm sure I still would have irritated the fuck out of Shelly.

She just kind of rolled with it, even when we argued.

And did we ever argue.

31. EARTHQUAKE ALERT!

Getting and keeping that auto parts delivery job was a big deal for me. It meant I got to drive a company car. It meant I had an answer when people said, "What do you do for a living?"

For a guy who had typically avoided any kind of structure where I had to follow instructions and report to someone, this was a great leap forward. I was proud as hell. To have that 10-bucks-an hour, 40-hour-a-week job and be able to hold on to it—that was victory. For the first maybe three months, every time I sat down behind the wheel of that company car, I felt like I'd won the lottery. After Folsom, driving around town and getting paid 10 dollars an hour to do it really can feel like you've hit the jackpot.

In between auto deliveries, I would stop at every comic shop and toy store I knew to check out what was new and interesting, talk about comics and buy comics. That's what kept me on track, kept me focused. The sense of being focused was important to my recovery and to my personal commitment to keep on living a (somewhat) normal existence.

I knew I wanted something more than delivering auto parts and collecting comic books, but I kept myself down. I didn't think I was capable of anything more in my life, I didn't think I was smart enough. I didn't think I had the skills. I assumed I would never get the money. I assumed I would never amount to much of anything. This was a bullshit way to think, especially in sobriety.

Sometimes when you're taking things "one day at a time", you confuse boredom with stability. At this point in my life, I thought humdrum was what I needed in order to stay sober. Maybe in the early days it was, but if

I had been honest with myself, I would have admitted I still had a whole lot of work to do, and I wasn't doing it.

Also, there was an arrogance about going to meetings that set in after I got married. It sort of snuck up on me, the thought that I was pretty much done, that I had the recovery thing figured out. At some point, it took over my head and I was just going through the motions. I was leading a normal life for the first time. Surely that meant most of the work was done now, right?

Wrong. If I'd been open and honest in the meetings (or anywhere else) about what I was feeling, that would have been obvious in a heartbeat. Yes, I had this moment: *Wow, it's possible—I was right. It's actually possible to live like a normal fucking human being.* That part was great. But I also had this moment: *Something's missing...something big.*

Even though I was sometimes going to two or three meetings a day, I didn't try to figure out *what* that gap was and how (or if) I could fill it. It surprises some people to learn, but even three meetings a day is not enough if you're not doing the right work. Even three meetings a day is no protection against going through the motions.

Pro tip: if you ever find yourself just going through the motions at the meetings, get ready for the fucking earthquakes.

32. THE SUPER BOWL THING

My dad and I had had a pretty horrible relationship as I was growing up, but when I got out of Folsom, my mom, dad, sister and I kind of mended fences. We got really close, and the strangest thing happened: I started having a good times with my dad.

Well, not always. We still got on each other's nerves, but we would go golfing a lot. Stuff like that. When we did that kind of thing, we'd be able to forget about getting on each other's nerves for a while. Suddenly, my dad was my golfing buddy, and that made sense. For both of us.

The other big bonding thing was Chargers games. My dad had season tickets for the San Diego Chargers, and we went to all the games, so we were able to connect over football, too. Even when we were hating on each other, we would be able to bond over the Chargers. One of us could say "*You suck!*" and the response would be, "*Yeah, well, you suck, too...but did you see what Dan Fouts did?*" Followed by, "*Yeah, that was amazing!*"

The 1994 season was good to Chargers fans, and the playoff games were even better. Against the odds, our Chargers made it to the Super Bowl.

This was a big fucking deal for me and my dad. We never, ever thought we'd see this. So we got ourselves tickets to the Super Bowl. We booked a flight. We booked a hotel. And we went out to Florida.

We turned the Big Game into a father-son trip, and we had the time of our lives, in person, at Super Bowl XXIX. The 49ers kicked the shit out of our team, but we didn't care. We weren't even supposed to be there, so we were elated. We made some great memories together on that trip.

Then, on the flight back, after we got done dissecting the game from every possible angle, after I thought we'd run out of stuff to talk about, my dad drained half the Diet Coke in the little tiny plastic cup they give you on airplanes, shook the ice in it to wake me up, because he thought I was about to drift off (which I wasn't), set the little tiny plastic cup down and asked me, "How are you and Shelly doing?"

Where did that come from? I thought this was a football trip.

"We're fine, Dad."

The conversation seemed to be over and nothing happened for a while. The stewardess came by and we handed her our tiny plastic cups that used to have Diet Coke in them. She put them in a white plastic sack and moved onto the next aisle. I wished that I could doze off, but I hated flying, and I kept thinking about my dad's seemingly random question.

That was random, right?

33. THE CONVENTION CONFUSION

Shelly and I weren't fine. Things had been getting steadily worse between us. We'd been fighting a lot, and the cycle was only accelerating.

The turning point was probably her freakout over the so-called porn convention trip. To understand why Shelly had a paranoid episode about me supposedly attending a porn convention, which is the next part of this story, you probably need to understand the ongoing, escalating argument that she and I had been having for years. That argument was all about my boxes and boxes of comic books.

At first, there didn't seem to be any argument at all. At the beginning, Shelly was cool with me buying comic books and even cool with me having a whole lot of them. It wasn't an issue. She knew collecting was one of the things I liked to do. She knew that before we got married.

Comic books in boxes became a big issue later, though, when money got tight. At this point, a narrative emerged on her side that I was spending "all our money" on collecting comic books and toys. In actual fact, I was spending maybe 50 to 70 bucks a month on this kind of thing, which didn't seem excessive to me. In fact, it seemed totally appropriate. As far as hobbies go, you could even say it was one of the cheaper options. The way I saw it, I was motivated to keep working hard *because* of the comic books. They were my reward *for* working hard, sometimes at two jobs.

This conversation continued, and it got more and more intense. It got to a point where I was constantly hearing some variation on: "Yeah, but it's not what grownups do. Anyway, you've got more than enough comic books."

I would try and keep it light, and maybe even make it funny, with a quip like:

"That's not really a thing—'Having more than enough comic books.'"

Her response would be something like:

"You think that's funny? It's not funny. What the hell's the point of spending good money on more and more copies of *Spider-Man*? You've got dozens of them, *hundreds* of them. Reread the ones you've got. Why should we be stacking up box after box after box of them?"

Then, one day, I said, "Who knows? I might want to open up a comic book store someday."

(*Wow. Where did that come from?*)

Shelly looked confused and a little disgusted. She shot back with, "Someday you're going to *what?*"

Now, here's the thing: Leaving the starting-a-comic-book-store thing aside, which was not much more than a daydream at that point, collecting stuff I loved was an obsession that I enjoyed. It was something I couldn't see any reason to apologize for. I'd always considered collecting comic books and toys part of my recovery.

Meaning: Not only could I order a Grand Slam at Denny's, but dammit, I could also stockpile comic books and collectibles. Collecting, as I saw it anyway, was one of the big reasons to *stay out of prison*. It was something I loved, something I couldn't possibly have done in Folsom. So it seemed to me like something I had coming and something I should keep doing.

Shelly, on the other hand, thought my collecting was a waste of not just money but time, space and attention. She kept hitting this point that collecting comic books was the opposite of "becoming a grownup." Whatever the fuck that was.

She was making a lot of assumptions about my desire to adhere to the prevailing standards of adult normalcy.

Now, once this issue came up as a big conflict point for us, there was no escaping it. Not only that: There was no compromise. No give and take. No back and forth. No attempt from Shelly to wean me off my comic-book addiction. It was all or nothing, black and white, right now. I *had* to agree that I wasn't going to buy comic books and collectibles any more, period. This was Shelly's line in the sand, so to speak.

144

Which means this is where things really began to go haywire.

I started covering up behaviors that I knew Shelly wouldn't approve of. I pretended to agree with her after she "laid down the law." I lied. I insisted that I had stopped buying comic books and toys…then I went out and bought more of them. Remember what I said earlier about not doing the work I should have been doing in meetings? This is a prime example. I airbrushed over all this stuff and just didn't deal with it. Not being honest is addict behavior.

Eventually, I realized that what I was doing was bullshit. It didn't make any sense to be lying and hiding comic books in places where she couldn't see them. This was who I was. It was time to stand my ground. I told Shelly flat-out that I wasn't going to stop collecting, and things went nuclear from there. Trust in the relationship pretty much collapsed.

I spent less and less time at home. Around the same time, a buddy of mine and I started working on a new project: a comic book. We had 1000 copies printed up and everything.[42] As you might imagine, Shelly wasn't a big fan of this side project…which is why I didn't ask permission or anything when my buddy and I decided it would be a great idea for me to head down to Vegas and start promoting our book at a comic convention that was happening there. I just did it.

Now, here's the thing: the convention, where we had a booth, was oversold. There were so many exhibitors that they had to set up an overflow wing out in a huge parking lot adjoining the convention center. Right *next* to the section of the parking lot devoted to the comic convention, there was a different kind of convention happening—a convention for the adult film industry.

A big black curtain separated the two events. It was a stupid idea, putting an adult film event right next to a comic book convention, and the organizers had a problem with kids from the comic book convention trying to sneak past the black curtain. *But*—and this next part is important—it wasn't *my* idea. I was there for the comic books.

Someone—to this day, I have no fucking idea who it was—called Shelly and told her that I was making the rounds at a porn convention. This was *not* the case, but when I got home, all of my stuff was packed up and arranged in neat stacks by the door and several of those stacks were my towers of comic book boxes.

"What the hell is this?" I asked. "What's going on?"

"You're moving out," Shelly said. "That's what's going on."

It took me an hour and a half to convince her I hadn't been cavorting with porn stars in Vegas, and she took me back. But things were not good between us. Even though I'd managed to negotiate a truce, and even though it was a relief not to have to find someplace else to stay that night, there was part of me that wasn't so sure I *wanted* to be taken back. There was this lighthouse in the back of my mind that kept up a soft but steady and niggling beacon: *This is not fucking working. This is not fucking working.*

I kept it together with Shelly, though (or tried to—because I thought that's what grownups were supposed to do). I wanted to do the adult thing and stick it out.

34. WE RUN OUT OF CHARGERS STUFF

Suddenly, my dad got cancer. And when cancer hit him, it didn't take long for me to figure out that this disease was not fucking around. It meant business.

This was a brutal, slow, horrible, painful decline, and it was hard to even witness what it was doing to him. Dad was a big man at six foot two, and quite portly. He kinda looked like a husky Roy Orbison. He had this booming voice and was very lively and social. He was the kind of guy who was loved by his clients. Then, overnight, it seemed, he withered away. He became a gaunt and pale version of himself.

It was just as hard to watch what cancer was doing to my mom, who didn't even have it.

My mom had been a caregiver for her sick father, and then a caregiver for her sick mother, and then a caregiver for my sick dad. She spent maybe a decade and a half taking care of sick family members, and because she was a human being who could only take so much, that completely fucked up her brain.

I'm not going to sugar-coat it: she never quite came back from that long tour of duty. Some people will tell you that what doesn't kill you makes you stronger. I'd like to point out that that saying doesn't allow for shit like cancer and C-PTSD, and whoever said it didn't see the shit my mom had to go through. Cancer didn't make my dad any stronger while he was with us, and dealing with it didn't make my mom any stronger. And I am here to tell you that C-PTSD may not kill you, but it sure as hell doesn't make you stronger or better equipped to deal with a close family member's terminal illness. Getting good *therapy* for C-PTSD can make you stronger, but that's a whole different topic.

As hard as it was to face him, I would go and visit my dad in the hospital. If I was there, my mom would feel like she could take a break… and I knew she needed a break. One day while I was visiting, my dad and I talked about the Chargers for a while, and when I closed my eyes, I could almost imagine for a moment that this was like any other day for us. But when I opened them, I was reminded it wasn't.

As the day went by, we ran out of Chargers stuff to swap opinions on, and the conversation hit a lull. Finally, my dad, who had been staring up at the ceiling for a while, said, "Shelly isn't making you happy."

It wasn't a question, and it wasn't an accusation. It was nothing he wanted me to confirm or deny. It was just a statement of fact.

Oh, so it's going to be like that? I thought. *You get to tell me about how to live my* life *now? Is* that *what we're doing?* But something inside kept me from saying it. To this day, I have no idea what that something was, but I'm glad I didn't say anything, because maybe 30 seconds later, he looked at me—apparently we were still doing this, whatever the hell it was—and added: "She doesn't even understand who you are."

He's right, I thought. *She has absolutely no fucking idea.*

Another 30 seconds went by, then another and another. Eventually, he said, "No one would blame you if you moved on. Your marriage isn't working."

I took that in and absorbed it, adding it to the thought pile. *Damn, he's right about that too. It isn't working.*

I didn't make any decisions about what I was going to do or not do. That wasn't the point of our conversation—and yes, it was a conversation, even though I wasn't saying anything. Instead, I just accept the moment: Shelly has no goddamned idea who I am, the marriage isn't working and my dad has been right about stuff, some of which was pretty damn important.

Cancer had managed to land a sucker punch on all of us, as a family. While the whole thing was horrible, the very worst part was that my dad went into remission. For a while, everything looked great, and we all thought we were off the hook. It seemed like we'd caught a huge break, and we all started feeling hopeful. We didn't know this was just cancer finding another, more interesting way to fuck with us, because it came back with a vengeance.

My dad went from being lucid, in remission, able to communicate and connect with people and on the rebound to getting his ass kicked as thoroughly as any human ass could possibly be kicked. That shift happened in just four or five weeks, and they were the worst weeks of the whole experience, by far.

I was there with him the last few days. So was my sister, and, of course, my mom. Near the end, my sister and I were kind of trading off care shifts; Dad was out of the hospital, doing hospice at home because we'd run out of options. There were no more treatments to be administered, just adjustments. The whole thing now was about trying to keep him as comfortable as we could.

He did have a nurse there to take care of him, and he had us, but the pain made him restless. He'd wake up and moan and we'd drip some morphine on his tongue to help him manage the pain. Then, one day, he was just gone.

And I was reeling, losing altitude fast.

Part of me knew I hadn't been doing anywhere near enough work in the meetings, and now, everything was so fucking terrible all at once that I felt like I would never possibly catch up. The only thing I knew with any certainty was that I needed a change. If things didn't change, life would get even uglier than it already was. And it was already pretty fucking ugly.

***

So, after seven years together, Shelly and I split up. They weren't all terrible years, but parts of them were pretty bad. My dad had been right: she had no idea who I was. More likely than not though—*way* more likely than not, in fact—she would probably say the same about me. Somehow, knowing that made the decision easier.

35. TURNING THE PAGE

Melissa and I had been friends when we were teenagers, years before I went to prison, and before I started my first-hand inspection of the California penal system, she and I had gone out. It was an off-and-on thing that had never amounted to much, because I was not the most stable guy at the time.[43]

Melissa had reached out to another old friend, and also to me, through this website called classmates.com. If you're of a certain age, you may remember how important it was around the year 2000. It was one of the very first digital connecting points, an early case study in online social engagement from that weird span of time when we were all apparently sitting around waiting for Facebook to be invented.

The point being, Melissa and I started emailing at the time, at first out of nostalgia and curiosity. We were sharing memories from my less-than-sterling academic career and catching up on everything that had happened to each of us since those days—our lives since *Rocky Horror*.

She wanted to know what I had been up to since we'd gone our separate ways and seemed fascinated to learn I was holding down a job delivering auto parts. She was happy I was working regularly, but she said it didn't sound like me. She was right: it didn't. She didn't seem particularly surprised about me going to Folsom (word had gotten around about that). She also didn't seem very surprised to learn I had gotten out and started going to AA meetings.

I was just as curious—fascinated, even—to learn what she'd been doing with *her* life. Melissa was now an upscale hairdresser and a sought-after hair colorist. Since we'd last connected, she'd apparently picked up some pretty heavy experience in the beauty industry. She was the creative director of a huge, swanky salon in downtown San Francisco.

A lot of emails went back and forth with updates like that. We were just buds, mutually curious about how things were working out. She was recently separated, and I was still married, but it didn't take long for us to figure out that things hadn't gone particularly well in *either* of our marriages (so eventually, we had that in common, too).

Melissa was very supportive about my dad's passing, which of course I appreciated. She spent some time emailing me about funny dates that she had been on—what it was like to be dating again, what had gone well on a given date and what hadn't, that kind of thing. Most of what we had in common, though, was a love of movies, TV shows and stories that made a difference. Tarantino was a shared obsession.

When things started falling apart for good with Shelly, I was in pretty bad shape. I decided it would be good for my mental health for me to take a trip up to San Francisco with some of our mutual friends to hang out with Melissa.

It was great hanging out in real life; my face hurt the next day from laughing and smiling so much. Then, via email, Melissa told me that her face hurt too for exactly the same reason.

We kept in touch.

I felt like I was turning a page.

36. "GO FOR IT"

We visited again when she came down to San Diego to see her dad, and she brought her son with her. We all had a fun time together, playing mini golf and eating tacos.

On one of our friendly visits, she and I went out to dinner. Everything felt easy and familiar and the conversation just flowed; it was great to talk to someone who not only got my quirky sense of humor but actually seemed to appreciate it.

It wasn't until we were leaving the restaurant that things began to feel a little strange between us. It had gotten dark, and we were walking along the beach to get back to the car. All at once, something hit me, something I had been thinking about for a while, something I just *knew* all of a sudden, from someplace deep down inside, that I needed to tell her right *now*. Let's just say that things had started to look a little different under the moonlight.

I looked her right in the eye.

"I wanted to say this next part, ah, face to face."

But then I stopped talking. Suddenly, this all felt awkward.

"Well?" Melissa said, alternately looking at me and out at the water. "Say what face to face?"

Nothing came out. There was a little smile on her face now that said: *I won't bite...* but still I couldn't manage to get it out.

"Say what?" she continued. "Something you couldn't put in an email? Okay, spit it out, Buechler."

"I just wanted to let you know that, ah...I know I was a crap boyfriend. Back in the day. I'm realizing I never really took you on a proper date."

"Yeah," she said, nodding slowly. "You were. You really were pretty terrible."

"And I wanted you to know: I'm so, so sorry about that."

She kept nodding, and she kept looking at me. There was a puzzled look on her face now. I got the feeling she was trying to figure out whether I meant it, or this was just something I'd felt obligated to say. Something I had to check off a list. A step that I needed to complete.

Fortunately, I did mean it.

So, no surprise, I made a lot more trips up to San Francisco. More and more weekends, I just seemed to find myself up there. Hanging out with Melissa was part of that—okay, a *big* part of that—but there was something else, too.

San Francisco had nerd culture woven deep into its DNA, and you saw evidence of it practically everywhere you went. San Diego was a sportier place, full of surfers and people in the military. I started to realize that I'd always been on the periphery there.

In San Francisco, if you knew Tolkien's *Lord of the Rings* books pretty well, which I did, and you loved to talk about them, which I did, the odds were pretty good that the next person you met either knew those books about as well as you did or, and this is the important part, *wanted to know why they mattered so much to you.* Either way, that person would tend to think it was cool how much you knew about Tolkien, how much Tolkien mattered to you. They would actually *enjoy* talking about Tolkien with you.

You were way less likely to run into someone like that in San Diego. In San Diego, it was far more common for the average person to think you were a bit bizarre for knowing that much about Tolkien. San Diego didn't celebrate people who obsessed about such things, but San Francisco did. I'm not just talking about Tolkien, of course, but about whatever your obsession of choice was: *Star Wars*, Spider-Man, the Dark Knight, *Watchmen*, Guns N' Roses, whatever. If you had taken the time to learn all there was to know about something you really, really loved, it made you someone worthy of respect in San Francisco.

In San Diego, it made you part of a fringe group of weirdos.

On one of my weekend visits, I told Melissa, "So I'm planning a move to San Francisco."

She gave me a wide-eyed look, a look that said, *What?! Did I miss something?*

"Wait, what? You're moving *here?*"

"Yeah."

"Why's that?"

"So we can spend more time hanging out. I mean, it's not like you could move to San Diego. Your clientele is here. Your son's school is here, and I like it here. I fit in."

She thought that over for a while, as though she were trying to figure out an unexpected math problem without writing anything down on paper. Then, after the wheels inside her head had turned maybe five or six times to check all the possible outcomes, she nodded like what I'd just said might just make sense. Like that surprised her.

"Okay," she said. It wasn't like I had asked for her permission or anything, but somehow it all felt more real when she agreed this was maybe a good idea. "Okay."

"Okay, then."

"You'll be happier here," she said. "It *is* a better fit. You will be appreciated here in a way that you would never be in San Diego. You're a creative guy, Gary. San Francisco is a better city to be creative in. You could really live up to your potential here—and nothing against San Diego, but how interesting is anyone who just spends their whole life in their hometown?"

The whole time I had been with Shelly, she had never once suggested that we make a big decision—or any decision—with the aim of either of us getting better, contributing more or elevating ourselves. But that's how Melissa was looking at this—as an opportunity for me to be happier and express myself creatively. The move, as she saw it, had the advantage of launching us both into a new adventure.

She looked me right in the eye and said, "Go for it."

Now, the wheels were starting to turn in *my* head: *Jesus, she's right. I can create something here. But what the hell am I supposed to create?*

37. THE NERD TALL DISCUSSION

Initially, the plan was for me to stay with Melissa for a few weeks while I found a place of my own—but it didn't quite turn out that way. I did come up on one of my weekend visits and started going through listings to look for an apartment, but I noticed Melissa was checking out what I was doing on the computer and she looked kind of dubious.

I looked up and said, "What is it?"

"Apartment sites? Really?"

"Yeah. What?"

"Look, you do what you want to do. You can get your own place if you want, but we both know that you're never going to be there."

Again, she was right. It had become obvious by now that we were both in pretty deep. And it was working. Which was great.

"There is somebody we need to talk to, though." Melissa said.

Which brings us to a truly awesome person I need to bring into the picture. We can call him Nerd Tall, his nickname in real life, though he wasn't very tall at the time since he was just five years old.

Nerd Tall was Melissa's son from her first marriage, and I had really come to adore Melissa's little boy. His bio dad wasn't really in the picture, and to me, it always seemed like this was for the better (but I'm not going to bore you with all the custody details).

As I said, Nerd Tall was still just a little guy when I decided to move up to San Francisco, and initially we were initially a little concerned about how he would respond to the new living arrangement. It was a lot for a child to take in. He was still in the single digits, after all. We were both concerned that he might feel a little left out or a little lost.

We didn't want that, so we took him out to our favorite neighborhood pizza place to talk it over. The three of us sat down at the table to order our usual pizzas, and I put a song on the jukebox—something by Sublime. The three of us chatted for a little while about music, and he told his mom about some stuff that had happened at school that day.

Then finally, Melissa said, "Listen, we want to talk to you about something."

"Oh yeah?" he replied. "What?"

"Well, Gary is going to move up to San Francisco so we can hang out together more. So, I was thinking that, maybe, he could move in with us. How does that sound to you?"

Nerd Tall thought for a second. Then, he nodded and said, "Oh, okay. Hey, why do you think the pizza is taking so long? I'm starving."

Things just got easier from there.

Some days, Melissa would say, "I'm looking for something fun to do with Nerd Tall." And I'd say, "Oh, I should take him to the zoo." Sometimes we'd all go, and sometimes he and I would have our own adventures. I liked having a little buddy to explore my new city with, and Nerd Tall was a smart kid who knew his way around, too. You could see he enjoyed showing me the ropes of urban life. He also became obsessed with...Spider-Man. Great, right?

Gradually, I started to realize that having kids meant being able to revisit all the good stuff about *being* a kid. That hadn't even occurred to me before.

38. CLICKING

Funny story about my first night moving into Melissa's place: we got robbed.

I had brought one big carload of stuff to get me started on my new life. It had been exhausting packing and then making the long drive, so that night, I slept like a rock. I maybe heard a little something going on in another room, but I figured it was somebody's late-night potty break.

It wasn't a kid though—it was a hot prowl job (meaning the guys who broke in did it *while we were home*). We didn't realize what had happened until the next morning. Once I figured out what had happened, it reminded me of when I'd broken into that guy's house the night I got busted for the first time.

Back then, I hadn't *meant* to go out on a hot prowl job. These guys, apparently, had; they must have been watching us move stuff in. They must've seen the lights go out before finding a way to unlatch a back door from the outside. They took all the money in Melissa's purse and stole my backpack.

I was the guy who called the police—me, the guy who'd hidden underneath a car and nearly gotten my head blown off by a retired sharpshooter. It was me on the phone, reporting it.

"Hi, officer, I need to report a robbery."

Karma's a bitch, right?

We were pissed, but of course, it could have been a lot worse. Nobody got hurt; all we lost was stuff.

We never got the stuff back because the cops never caught up with them, but I couldn't manage too much righteous indignation. I figured I had maybe moved a little bit closer to evening up the Big Scoreboard of Life.

I settled in at Melissa's, but we both knew more changes were on the horizon, because Melissa's lease would be up in about eight months. But those eight months flew by, and once they did, we started looking at houses.

There weren't many places we could afford in the city, so it was a pretty short house-hunting expedition, though fortunately we found a place we liked. Six months after we bought that house, we were engaged—and six months after that, we got married.[44] It didn't feel like things were moving too fast; it felt like things were *clicking*.

We both felt like we'd wasted so much time on people who didn't appreciate us that we didn't want to waste another minute. It was full steam ahead into a new life together. We were catching up on everything we'd been missing. It was intoxicating.

When I lived in San Diego, I learned how to turn wrenches. I'd stopped working as a delivery driver, and for a while, I was a mechanic. Truth be told, though, I hated that line of work. So, I got another auto parts job.

The money was good. The benefits were good. The new job had a lot of social contact and, of course, I'm a very social person. Things were looking up at last: I was with the right woman, I loved my new little family and I liked my work. Life was pretty good. The job wasn't that hard, and *wow*, I wasn't getting any grief at home anymore about collecting comics.

So that's what I did. My favorite comics shop, my go-to spot, was this little store out on Ocean Avenue called The Comic Outpost. I could (and did) spend hours in there, and I wasn't the only one.

The place was always busy, which I loved; it was easy to talk to people who loved comics as much as I did. It was a gathering spot and meeting place, and something about the store and the people who hung out there really sang to me. It all made me feel welcome—*safe*, even. The Comic Outpost became my single favorite place to get my comics, graphic novels and superhero-collectibles fix. Before long, it was the *only* place I went to get my fix.

If you happen to be in recovery, and you're the kind of person who's going to be hooked on *something*, let me take this opportunity to point out that comic books are probably your best option for a replacement addiction. Think about it: massive stress relief, but no physical or mental health risks…

…great stories to inspire you and keep you going, assuming you buy the right stuff…

…positive social interactions with fellow comic addicts at conventions and places like the Comic Outpost, my go-to spot in San Francisco.

What's not to like?

The Comic Outpost, was where I always went for my weekly comics fix. For me, it was San Francisco at its very best: eclectic, connected and up-to-date while at the same time steeped in history and unapologetically nerd-friendly.

I bought a whole lot of books and toys there, and my collection expanded—dramatically—to over 150 cardboard boxes' worth of comics and related materials.

FOR ME, THOSE 150-PLUS CARDBOARD BOXES MEASURED OUT THE DISTANCE BETWEEN WHAT I CONSIDERED REALITY... AND WHAT MORE_WHAT'S THE WORD I'M LOOKING FOR HERE? "NORMAL"? "TRADITIONAL"? "LESS OBVIOUSLY DAMAGED"?_ PEOPLE THOUGHT OF AS REALIT

BY THIS POINT, I HAD DECIDED THAT I WAS FINE WITH MY DEFINITION OF REALITY:

THAT'S WHAT EXISTS. THAT'S WHAT'S REAL

WHAT'S REAL IS WHAT GETS YOU THROUGH THE NIGHT SOBER.

THOSE 150 BOXES CONTAINED EVERY COMIC BOOK, EVERY GRAPHIC NOVEL THAT HAD GOTTEN ME THROUGH FOLSOM, AND EVERY BOOK I HAD COLLECTED SINCE GETTING OUT. I WAS PROUD OF EVERY FUCKING ONE OF THOSE BOXES.

PART FOUR:
FEAR AND LOATHING

In Part Four, I marry Melissa, buy a comic book store in San Francisco, work like a maniac to make sure it succeeds and gradually stop going to meetings. Surprise, surprise: I relapse. Also: I fixate on pop culture.

39. "WE HAVE ISSUES"

Was the stuff in all those cardboard boxes escapism? Sure. I was cool with that. Life gives each of us plenty to escape from. The stupid move would have been *not* escaping from the shit that was about to overwhelm me. Comics—and movies and TV shows and novels and games—gave me an escape route. I had no problem with any of that. We all needed a break now and then.

When I'd told Shelly all my boxes were inventory for a comic book store I was thinking about opening someday, she'd looked at me like I needed to be locked up somewhere. When I told Melissa the same thing, she said: "Do it! I'm not kidding, you should do that. Why wait until you're old to do what you dream of doing? Go for it."

Interesting. Very different response. Very different person. Very different set of priorities. Then, a couple months down the line, I found out The Comic Outpost was for sale.

I had some money in the savings account that my dad had left me. Was I crazy, or was this the right move? Should I leave my auto parts job and its good salary, walk away from the benefits and actually *buy* this place? Was *this* what I was supposed to do next? Was *this* what I was supposed to create?

My gut was saying yes.

Melissa's instincts said yes, too. I was expecting more resistance, but she was all in.

"That kind of flexibility might be really good when we have a baby," she said. We had always planned on having a baby at some point. "I mean, obviously I'm going to keep working after our baby's born. If there's an emergency, and I'm in a situation where I can't leave a customer because I've got chemicals all over someone's head or something, we'd have a lot more options if you were doing something like running a comic shop. Whenever you needed to, you could leave someone else in charge or just put a sign on the door, close up shop for a while and then come back when the emergency was taken care of."

It was not the response I expected from her, but I loved what I was hearing.

"This would be an adventure," she went on. "I mean, I absolutely love what I do, and you deserve to have that feeling, too."

We made the decision together, which up to that point was the biggest decision of my life. We went for it. We bought the store.

Together, Melissa and I moved all 150-plus cardboard boxes out of storage and into the store we now owned. We kept the old name, The Comic Outpost, but we connected it to a brand new catch-phrase:

"We have issues."

And overnight, everything changed.

40. THE OTHER 10 PERCENT

There's a quote from the late, great Glenn Frey (the guy who sings lead on "Tequila Sunrise" and "New Kid in Town") that connects to what I'm about to give you. Frey says of his incredibly successful, deeply, deeply, deeply dysfunctional band: "Ninety percent of the time, being in the Eagles was a fucking blast."

Today, I know *exactly* where Frey was coming from when he said that. And I also know the flipside, the part he left unsaid: Sometimes, the other 10 percent sucks so bad that it overwhelms the good times. Sometimes, the other 10 percent kicks your ass in a dark alley like you owe it money.

I ran The Comic Outpost for 10 years, and the first eight of them were a fucking blast. But the last two years sucked ass, as a direct result of decisions I made when I not only should have known better but *did* know better. So, this next part is all about terrible choices.

I chose dysfunction. I hugged dysfunction close like it was my long-lost brother. I chose arrogance. I thought arrogance made me stronger and better. I chose not to work the program that had saved my life, because I thought I knew better than the program did. Basically, I stopped doing the work and started a countdown to relapse—and I knew exactly what I was doing every goddamn step of the way. I chose to stop going to meetings, and I knew, when I stopped going, that that was a major, major mistake.

So, listen: I'm going to focus on the part that was a fucking blast now, because those eight years are a legit part of the story and they're definitely part of who I am now—but as you read this, please do me a personal favor and consider what you see over the next pages to be the prelude to the much bigger, much more important story we'll get to next: *Don't stop doing the work. Don't stop going to the fucking meetings.* Because I wouldn't wish the other two years on my worst enemy.

***

Starting in 2003, when I took over The Comic Outpost, I had fun at work on a daily basis for the very first time in my life. That was a revelation. Every time it happened, I wanted to make it happen again, and I didn't let a lack of experience stop me. I saw my lack of experience as an advantage, as something that made it easier for me to do things other people were unwilling or unable to do.

> **"If you take any activity, any art, any discipline, any skill, take it and push it as far as it will go, push it beyond where it has ever been before, push it to the wildest edge of edges, then you force it into the realm of magic."**
>
> **–Tom Robbins**

Seriously, I had no business pretending to be an entrepreneur, because I had absolutely no idea what the fuck I was doing.

Fortunately, being an entrepreneur is the kind of job where if you *pretend* you know what you're doing, you stay flexible, you pay attention, you notice what works and what doesn't and you can survive financially for a couple of months in a row, you can actually end up getting significantly better at your job. You can't be an airline pilot, a brain surgeon, an air traffic controller or an ambulance dispatcher with that approach, but you *can* be an entrepreneur—and I'm proof of that.

I fell on my ass a lot. I kept getting up, kept looking for answers, kept trying to figure out what other people were doing in other stores that was working for them and might work for me. I kept going, which was definitely a change of pace for someone who had never, ever done that before in a work context.

The reason I kept going—kept devouring books about how to run a business, kept visiting comic stores in every city I could get to, kept making calls and kept making friends in the business, kept asking people about what worked and listening to the answers that came back[45]—was that *I had found my purpose in life*. I'd found my calling. Turns out I really, really loved connecting with people and talking with them about nerd stuff.

That's what I was all about: connecting in depth, and at length, about all the nerdy stuff. That was my purpose. That was what got me up early in the morning and kept me up late at night.

41. A PLACE WHERE NERDS FELT AT HOME

From day one, I considered the one-on-one relationships I had with customers to be the single most important thing about running a comic store.

That part never changed. I always wanted to know everybody's name as they walked in the door. I wanted to understand who they were, because my job was to match them to their story.

Because here's the thing: everybody's got a story. You do, I do, all of us do. So, you and I are going to talk, and we're going to connect, and at some point in the conversation, I'm going to figure out what makes you tick—what you like, what gets you going. Then, I'm going to match you to your story. Even if you walk in the door, we start chatting and you tell me you've never bought a comic book in your life, you and I are going to figure this out.

I'm going to be like, *Okay, what movies do you like? What TV shows do you like? What do you like to read?* And based on what you tell me, I am going to point you toward a comic book I think you'll like.

I got pretty good at that. Most of the time, I got it right.

Based on those discussions, hundreds of them—thousands of them, if I'm honest—people would give me a list of comic books of every new release they wanted. Then, I'd pull their books off the shelf before I even opened the store and set aside their issues in a little box, and they'd swing by during the day and pick up the comics. Those people were called subscribers.

When I took over, I had 16 of them. After I'd been up and running for a month, I had about 50, and it seemed like I was picking up more of them every day.

Subscribers were the lifeblood of the shop. I knew all their names. More and more, subscribers started not just dropping in to pick up their books but *hanging out* at the store. They stayed for the conversation, which I loved. It got to a point where we had to put in couches and chairs and vintage arcade games, because a lot of people would hang out all day. For me, that was a huge win. This wasn't one of those stores where you got rushed off the premises.

The Comic Outpost became a place where nerds felt at home. I knew, because I was one of them, and I felt safe there.

I loved the place. Just loved it.

As excited as I was about what was happening at the store, the reality was: it wasn't making any money...yet. On a good week, I broke even. But I didn't always have a good week. I was on the right trajectory, I could feel it, and I was having the time of my life. But I also knew that, if I let up, I would lose momentum, lose foot traffic, lose buzz, lose word of mouth, lose the trajectory, lose everything I had worked so hard to build up in the first year.

So I didn't let up.

Soon, I was working 16-hour days, seven days a week. The store was pretty much my life. Fortunately, Melissa understood about magnificent obsessions: she had her own magnificent obsession, and she wanted me to have mine. She wanted it to work, so things at home were cool for the most part. But working really long hours, day after day after day, meant it was getting harder to go to meetings.

My calls with Ballsack, my sponsor back in San Diego, were happening less and less often. Truth be told, he'd also seemed to be getting distracted, like there was something else going on in his world, something he didn't want to talk about. I didn't press the issue.

One night, when I came home from work way late (again) and crawled into bed exhausted, (again), Melissa (who'd been waiting up for me) kissed me on the forehead and said: "Hey, can I ask you something?"

"Sure," I said. "Just don't make it complicated. I've got nothing left, as in no more brain cells. As long as you don't ask me to solve a problem, and as long as it's light, ask away."

"Well, I don't really know how AA works, but...shouldn't you get a sponsor who lives in San Francisco? In addition to your old one, I mean. If something comes up, if there's a problem you have to deal with, wouldn't it be better to have someone you could talk to face to face? In person? Right away?"

It was a fair question. An important question. But I really didn't have the energy to deal with any of it. So I took the easy way out, the coward's way out. I bullshitted my wife. I kept her in the dark. I yawned, leaning into the exhaustion, which was genuine though I was making a point of emphasizing it, because I just didn't feel like talking.

"Well, you can, but you don't have to," I replied. "It's not a big deal. One sponsor is really all you need."

She nodded. Then maybe a minute later, she said: "When's the last time you talked to your sponsor though?"

I pretended I was already asleep, and she bought it. Or seemed to, anyway.

42. FUCK THE MAN

By the midpoint of Year Two, it was obvious I had something special going on at The Comic Outpost. There was nothing else like it in the city, and that was no accident. I'd looked closely at what else was happening in the market, and I'd chosen to do something different so I could do a better job of attracting and holding on to customers than other stores. That's capitalism, by the way, and it's pretty cool—when you don't fuck with it or use it to tell people how to make their decisions, think their thoughts and live their lives.[46]

When I took over The Comic Outpost, I knew there were a whole lot of comic book stores in the Bay Area, but I also knew that they all seemed to break down into one of two basic categories. The first bucket was what's known in the industry as a "Diamond newsstand," meaning a store that works with, Diamond Comic Distributors, the largest, most dominant worldwide distributor of English-language comic books, graphic novels and related merch.

If you're a Diamond newsstand, you're basically just filling in a template. You're following a middle-of-the-road, paint-by-numbers inventory, backed up by a middle-of-the-road, paint-by-numbers strategy for things like store layout and marketing. There's not a lot of room for personalization or creativity. You're trying to be all things to all people, and most of the time, you're probably succeeding with that model. It's a lowest-common-denominator store plan, a safe bet. I'm not knocking this approach, because it's a valid way to run a store—but it was the way The Man would run a store. That wasn't what I wanted to do. Fuck The Man.

If the first bucket was the Diamond newsstand, the other bucket was way, way different. These were the stores that went to the other extreme. I'm talking about the edgy, independent, in-your-face comic shops. Loud. Brash. Abrasive. Kind of a punk vibe, a vibe that leaned, at times, into more graphic, more intense adult material. I didn't want to do that, either, even though that's a perfectly valid model for a comic book store. It worked back then, especially in San Francisco, and it still works today—but it wasn't my thing.

My thing was more kid-friendly. Family-friendly. Normie stuff. The aesthetic I'd loved growing up: lots of heroes in tights, lots of bad guys for them to vanquish, all in a little four-color palace you could feel comfortable taking children to. The kind of store I could go to and feel comfortable bringing Nerd Tall along with me. Toys, yes, but mostly ones that connected directly to the comic books I loved. No Magic: The Gathering, no Yu-Gi-Oh!, no Dungeons and Dragons—nothing against those things, I just didn't know anything about them, so I wasn't going to build my store around them. Just comic books and toys that I loved, hand-selected and kid-friendly. That was my brand. That's what emerged at The Comic Outpost, and that's what ended up working.

Financially speaking, the store turned the corner. Foot traffic got better. The weeks where we made money became the norm, not the rare exception. That meant it wasn't just Melissa's job that was paying the mortgage and keeping the lights on. The store started doing that for our family, too, and yes, that meant a lot to me. So, I kept at it.

I was having a blast, all working day, every working day, which suddenly seemed like the most important thing at the time—that and paying the bills. Meanwhile, there I was, doing both of those things at the exact same time. Life was good.

Or...*could* have been good.

I wasn't going to meetings anymore. At all. I wasn't doing the work. I was being a workaholic, which is not the same thing.

One night, I came home from work way late (again), and crawled into bed exhausted (again), and Melissa (who'd been waiting up for me) kissed me on the forehead (again). Then, she said: "Hey, can I ask you something?"

"Sure, just no drama, okay? I'm all drama-ed out. It was a tough day today."

"I understand. I don't *think* this is drama, I just…"

"What? Sounds like drama."

"No, I was just curious about, you know…the last time you went to a meeting?"

"Jesus, really? At a quarter to midnight? This is *such* drama. I am all out of ammunition, sorry. Answer: a while. Okay? Please don't worry about this kind of stuff. Please. I've got this covered."

"Yeah?"

"Yeah."

"But, I mean—aren't you supposed to go to meetings?"

"Technically, yeah, and I will. It's just been really busy."

"I know."

With that, I turned over and started to drift off. After a minute or so, Melissa spoke again.

"Hey, you still awake?"

I pretended to be asleep, but she had gotten wise to me.

"Gary? You're awake, right?"

"Yeah."

"When was the last time you went to a meeting?"

I really do not need this at the end of a long day.

"*I'm* the one with the problem," I said finally. "*You're* not the one with the problem. I know how to handle this. I promise."

43. THE ECOSYSTEM

The tempo started picking up at the store.

There were a couple of overlapping reasons for that. Some of the increased foot traffic, visibility and dollar volume had to do with ideas that I was putting into play—but if I'm honest, a lot of it had to do with some big changes that were taking place in the media ecosystem The Comic Outpost was a part of.

Since having an opinion about media is pretty much my day job now, and since the changes in the media landscape that took place as the store became successful had a lasting impact on pretty much everyone, let's look at those first. After that, I'll brag about a couple of the ideas I threw out that ended up working.[47]

Okay. We're talking about the early 2000s. I took over the store in 2003 and I ran it for the next decade. This timespan coincided, fortunately for me, with a phase of media history in which superhero stories and properties became big, big business. This was a rising tide that lifted a lot of boats, and my little comic-book store on Ocean Avenue was definitely one of those boats. It's a point of pride to me that the three films that launched this global intensification of interest in superheroes and the classic comic franchises that gave rise to them were all directed by—here comes that word again—nerds.

Without the nerds, who knows what the hell might have happened.

With them, though, the way people thought about comic book heroes, movies and the intersection of those two things, about all the stuff that we would now call "content" but that back then didn't really have a name, changed dramatically—not just in the USA, but in most developed regions of Planet Earth. And there were three guys in particular who took the ecosystem to the next level.

In the decade that followed 9/11, three nerds put out work that engineered and sustained a major global thought-shift, and that thought–shift created increasing numbers of people willing to pay good money for comic books and associated merchandise. Those three nerds were:

Sam Raimi, the director and long-time Spider-Man superfan who worshipped his source material long enough and seriously enough to deliver the first Spidey film in 2002.

John Favreau, the director and long-time comics geek who worshipped his source material long enough and seriously enough to deliver the first *Iron Man* film in 2008. Yes, Favreau was eventually co-opted by people in suits who were waving large amounts of cash at him, but that phase came later. I'm talking about the nerd phase, the phase where he fought for, and won, the right to cast Iron Man superfan Robert Downey, Jr. in the title role.

Christopher Nolan, the director and long-time Batman superfan who worshipped his source material long enough and seriously enough to deliver *Batman Begins* in 2005 and its mindblowing 2008 sequel that made the rest of Hollywood look idiotic (not for the first or last time), *The Dark Knight.*

The impact of those three nerds[48] on the comic-book industry and on consumer media as a whole really can't be overstated. They loved their material, and it showed. People responded—worldwide.

> **Notice the pattern: love your source material, know it inside out, treat it with love and respect, treat the *audience* with love and respect and good things happen.**

I'm not going to lie. All three of those guys and the media blitz that accompanied each of their big hit films helped The Comic Outpost sell more stuff.

So that's the ecosystem shifting. That helped. Also, I had some guerilla marketing ideas.

The most important of these was the breakthrough idea of going the extra mile—just absolutely going for it if it would help a customer. This idea hit me at some point in Year Two. What if I did what no other owner of any other comic store would do to take care of my subscribers? What if I went above and beyond the call, every single time, for every one of them?

That seemed like a good idea. That seemed like a great way to stand out. I started down that road, and I never fucking looked back. Honestly, no customer request irritated me, ever, from that point onward. I would stay open an hour late for a customer. I would open early for a customer. Whatever they needed, I would find a way to do it. I would leave an employee in charge of the cash register and run home and get comics out of my own collection while the customer was waiting, then come back to the store with them just to make sure that they had a complete set of something they wanted.

People remembered that kind of thing. People liked that kind of thing and told their friends about it. Some people would call what I'm talking about here over-the-top. I call it good customer service.[49]

Another thing that helped was me finding more and more cool stuff I could put in the store environment that would help other nerds feel like they'd finally made it home, feel like they were welcome to stick around for as long as they wanted. I never stopped looking for that stuff, never stopped finding it and never stopped finding places in the store to put it, whatever that might happen to be.[50]

It worked. The nerds showed up. They stuck around. They told their friends. Their *friends* stuck around. And The Comic Outpost, at long last, got hot.

44. "DON'T TELL ME WHAT TO DO"

By this point, Melissa and I had a baby, a great little guy we now call Nerd Junior, so I'll call him that here. He's a beacon to my life, the lighthouse on the shore that I can always point myself toward.

Remember how, when Melissa and I were first bouncing around the idea of me buying the store, we thought it made more sense for me to work in retail so I'd have plenty of flexibility and would be able to help out with childcare and emergencies? Yeah, that didn't actually happen. By the time Nerd Junior came along, I was locked into an alternate universe called The Comic Outpost. There were occasional wormhole expeditions where I could cross from one timeline to another, but the flexibility thing never quite materialized the way Melissa had mapped out for us. That was a source of stress—one of many sources of stress in our relationship, if I'm honest.[51]

See, there was no shortage of things that were causing stress in my life. Meeting payroll. Keeping people motivated. Keeping customers coming through the door. Planning the next big marketing thing. All of that was stressful, so that whole issue of flexibility at home kind of had to get in line and wait its turn.

Any time something like that came up, any time *anything* of importance to another human being (or to me) came up that wasn't directly connected to what I was doing the next day at The Comic Outpost, I had this interesting response. I'd go, "Whoa, whoa, whoa—I've got stuff to deal with. So much to deal with. Tell you what: we'll get to that later, okay? I've got a store to keep afloat."

And of course, whatever it was, I never got back to it.

Flexibility was like that. Work-life balance was like that. Last but certainly not least, going to meetings was like that. I thought I was Superman. I thought I could just get back to all that stuff...eventually (or not). Maybe the problem would solve itself. That happens sometimes, right? Most of the time, I thought I could just turn the page and focus on what I wanted to do next. That's a very ADHD response to a major problem, by the way: *Turn the page, maybe it will go away.*

It doesn't work. But I hadn't learned that yet.

A big part of my problem was having an attitude, which can really be a double-edged sword, especially if you happen to be an entrepreneur: "Don't tell me what to do."

Now, for people who aren't entrepreneurs, or who don't happen to know an entrepreneur really well or live with one, I can see how that attitude might not seem like a double-edged sword at all. It might just seem obnoxious. But it's not. It's a major asset if you're trying to get a business off the ground and keep it flying. It backfires sometimes, sure, and you have to clean up after yourself now and then...but without "don't tell me what to do," without that framework for responding to challenges, entrepreneurial creativity and innovation and the best kind of obsession just do not happen.

Without "don't tell me what to do," I would have believed all those people telling me it was a stupid idea to buy a comic book store in the first place, or telling me not to open one unless it followed a business model an accountant could easily understand. Buying The Comic Outpost *wasn't* a stupid idea, and the spreadsheet models that accountants could figure out and generate variations on and write their little case studies about were no good for me. So in those situations, "don't tell me what to do" really was a totally constructive response.

There's also a dysfunctional, unworkable side to "don't tell me what to do." Try saying it to the IRS sometime, and you'll see what I mean. I'm a pretty smart guy, and I should have figured that out, but somehow, I found plenty of places to lean into "don't tell me what to do" when I really shouldn't have. The more of an obsession the store became for me—and it definitely was an obsession—the less energy and attention I had for things like AA meetings and working on my own shit. My own dysfunction, my own brokenness. And the brokenness wasn't going away just because I had a store to run.

Every time my sponsor, my friends from meetings, Melissa or anyone else tried to find ways to *tactfully* bring any of this to my attention, my instant, hair-trigger response was, "Don't tell me what to do." And that was toxic. Not just because of its impact on other people, including Melissa, but also because it was keeping me from getting the support I needed to maintain my sobriety.

I honestly didn't think I needed that support. I thought I had it all figured out. I thought the store was the answer. I actually thought I was getting better. I sold myself that story, a story that left me deeply vulnerable, blind to the personal and professional disaster I was headed toward, clueless about the nearness and steepness of the cliff I was about to drive off of.

I mean it. I had absolutely no idea how vulnerable I was.

One day, I got word from San Diego that Ballsack had fallen off the wagon and slashed his wrists in a holding cell instead of going back to San Quentin. He was gone.

There was a lot of speculation about how he got the razor, but I wasn't interested in any of those discussions. So, I disengaged. I didn't much feel like talking about him at all, frankly.

Or about AA.

Or about going to meetings.

After all, I had a business to run.

45. MY THUMB

I had always suspected a day would come when everything started to collapse around me. I now know exactly what day that was. It was the day I fucked up my thumb.

Let me be clear about something: I was delusional at this point in my life, just as delusional as I was when I decided it would be a great idea to break into my ex-girlfriend's dad's house. Back then, I thought I was invulnerable. Now, the delusion was even worse: I still thought I was invulnerable, but I also thought I was an adult. Because the store was finally up and running, I guess.

In reality, I was still a little kid inside—picture a little kid playing with, like, power tools or something, or pushing buttons at random in the control room of a nuclear reactor, totally unsupervised. Or, in my case, picture a little kid playing with a ladder, getting ready to hang up a huge *Superman Returns* banner (it had just come out, and we were setting up the store for a big promo push on all Superman stuff).

There were these really high ceilings in The Comic Outpost, so you had to get way up there when you were going to hang up or take down a big banner, which was something we did pretty regularly. And we had this giant ladder on hand for this kind of job. It was something I'd done many times, something I almost did on autopilot. But it's those autopilot moments that you have to watch out for.

My assistant and I were hanging up our massive vinyl *Superman Returns* banner using our giant folding ladder. I was all the way up there and I thought the ladder was steady, but it wasn't. I shifted my weight, and the moment I shifted, *time* shifted. Everything slowed down for some reason.

I heard the ladder give a little creak that it wasn't supposed to give. It was supposed to be steady. It wasn't supposed to make any noise.

The ladder folded in on my thumb. Just crushed it flat.

I'd broken a bone in my thumb, though of course I didn't know that at the time. All I knew was my thumb hurt like hell. I shouted, tried to adjust, managed to disengage my thumb from the ladder that had just fucking bitten me—but as I did that, I lost my balance.

As I was shouting—as the sound of agony was still rising up from my lungs and out of my throat on account of my thumb being crushed and broken—I heard a weird sound right *under* the sound of my own voice.

It was a sound I really, really didn't like, one I didn't want to hear at all: the sound of the ladder giving way and sliding to one side underneath me because I'd shifted my weight.

I looked down, trying to gauge where the ladder was so I could shift it back into place, but instead of seeing the ladder, I saw the floor getting closer.

Somehow, I stopped shouting and thought to myself: *This isn't good. I've done this before. At my parents' house. Sneaking out that night. Anyway, I'm way the fuck up here, and this is going to hurt if I land wrong. It hurts like hell when you land wrong, I remember that. I need to be sure I land right.*

But I didn't have time to change the way I landed. Suddenly, without warning, time sped up again, and I hit the floor hard.

***

My assistant didn't know how to drive, so I had to drive myself to the emergency room. Imagine yourself behind the wheel of a car, with the worst pain you've ever experienced in your entire fucking life, coming at you from your flattened thumb.

The pain was just relentless. All the time I was navigating traffic, I was thinking: *If I get into a fucking accident on the way, that's just going to make things suck even worse, so let's pay attention to the road here and pretend all this information that my nervous system is sending me isn't happening.* But the whole way there, I had my pain stereo up at a Spinal Tap level of 11 out of 10 and no way to turn down the dial.

It was an interesting ride. Truthfully, I don't know how I kept it together. It kind of felt like someone else was driving, actually, but I was the only one in the car.

Whoever it was behind the wheel, that trip seemed to take forever.

***

I finally made it to the emergency room, and the doctors there were impressed: it looked to me like they hadn't seen a case quite like this before. I begged them to cut the thumb off, but they wouldn't do it. Instead, they drilled a hole right through the thumbnail and put a little pin in. That was fascinating to watch. The blood squirted out like fucking Monty Python.

I was in agony. Absolute agony. I had broken bones before. I had gotten concussions. I'd been knocked out. I'd had teeth knocked out. I'd broken my tailbone. Nothing hurt as much as my thumb being flattened. It was the worst.

Before they let me out of the emergency room, though, they handed me some Vicodin, which worked wonders—until it wore off.[52]

They'd given me a vial containing 10 of those little pills in the emergency room, and I took them as prescribed, to take the edge off the pain. I took it at a time when I really was dealing with a lot of physical pain, pain with a mean fucking left hook.

Yes, I still considered myself on the path, in recovery, sober, as I took those 10 pills "as needed" for the pain I was managing. But when I got done with the 10, that evil left hook was still alive and well, so I got a prescription for some Oxycontin. Google that word "Oxycontin" when you get the chance—it's good for a chuckle.

I'm not going to get too political here, but for the sake of keeping it real, I do have to tell you that the stuff doctors were prescribing to people like me at that time was a hell of a lot more addictive than anyone let on at the time—and doctors were being pressured to prescribe it a hell of a lot more than they should have been. Like I said, if you don't already have a history with Oxycontin, or know someone who does, Google it. You'll laugh. You'll cry. You'll connect the dots.

I took the Oxycontin and I told myself I was fine. I told myself I could handle it. I told myself I was still sober.

Wrong, wrong and wrong.

46. MY NEW HOBBY

Two weeks after that incident with the ladder, I was off to the fucking races. By that point I was taking Oxycontin at a pace that not even I could pretend was healthy. So no, I was no longer pretending I was sober.

Fourteen days in, I *knew* I wasn't sober anymore. My focus now was on *covering up* the fact that I wasn't sober, from Melissa and from the rest of the world. And the button I pushed to dominate the necessary conversations to achieve that goal was a familiar button: "Don't tell me what to do."

I was a man on a mission, and the mission was: *Don't own up.* That's a big shift from being in recovery and believing you're sober. That's a lot of bullshit to swallow. It's hard to do that without an excuse to justify your own behavior. Addicts are good at excuses, though, and that's what I was again: an addict, one who had relapsed.

The excuse I used to justify all of my bullshit was that I needed to get back up on my feet and operational so I could get back to running the store and supporting my family. And for that, obviously, I needed pain relief. Right? Right.

Not long after the accident, even though I was downing Oxycontins like they were Tic-Tacs, I figured I could probably use some more pain relief, so I got hold of some more Vicodin (I'd really liked that stuff). I got Vicodin under the table, from a friend who had a reliable supply and agreed to mail me the pills. Because again, you know—I needed that to get back up on my feet and operational. And, apparently, I also needed some propellants.

Don't look now, but I decided this was also the perfect time to cultivate a serious cocaine habit.

It was easier to do than you might imagine, because when you run a comic book store, it's surprising how often people offer you free drugs. That kind of thing had been happening for years already, but the difference now, I was starting to say yes. I would take a break and bring some favored customer or other into a back room where we could snort in peace, without being judged by the other clientele. Pause here to sniff, wipe nose and check to see if any white powder is visible before we head back out to face the real world.

That coke didn't stay free for long, though. All of a sudden—and believe me when I say time got a bit wobbly here, because, no shit, to me it *really* seemed like it happened overnight—I had a brand-new member of the family to support: my escalating, self-destructive and ever-more-expensive coke-and-pills hobby.

Bottom line: shit had officially gotten serious, and I knew that. But it was my job (as Addict Me saw it, anyway) to make sure Melissa never found out just *how* serious shit had gotten.

All right, here comes the hard part—the house-of-cards-collapsing part.

For full disclosure, I didn't much feel like writing this bit, but all kinds of shit we don't feel like doing turns out to be exactly what we need to do next. Subtext I really, really want you to hear as declared text: *Do not stop going to the fucking meetings.* Got that? Good. Okay, here we go. Strap in.

47. EVERY MAN FOR HIMSELF

Remember, at this point, Melissa and I have a little guy to take care of who is barely a toddler: Nerd Junior. Gary of the Broken Thumb can't wash any bottles, can't snap a onesie, can't help with bath time, can't buckle a car seat. Guess who had to do all that stuff? Of course: Melissa.

Even if I hadn't been as deeply committed as I was to rediscovering and channeling my Inner Asshole, those changes alone would have put Melissa into survival mode: handling every little thing at home, that came up with the baby and with Nerd Tall—while also (let's not forget) running her own business.

And, yes, to make matters way worse, every day, I was more and more in touch with my Inner Asshole. I was more of a pain to be around, more embedded in the task of living out *World's Worst Husband* (the sequel to my first big hit, *World's Worst Boyfriend*). That sequel sucks even worse than the original, by the way. I can't recommend that anyone sit through it. But, against all odds, she did.

Melissa was covering so much that she literally had to be treated for exhaustion. She had no strength left. She had to go to the doctor, who prescribed her plenty of rest. But how was that supposed to happen, exactly, with me inhaling Oxycontin? With me taking candy from strangers, snorting coke in back rooms, looking for excuses not to go home until the last possible moment?

The fact that I dismissed questions like these in smaller and smaller fractions of a second every single fucking time they crossed my mind will give you some sense of the state of our relationship. We were falling apart.

One night, I came home from work way, way, way late (as usual), crawled into bed exhausted (as usual) and turned over to avoid unnecessary conversation (as usual). Melissa, who by now had stopped kissing me on the forehead, said: "Hey, can I ask you something?"

I heard myself say: "Hey, what if you didn't?"

"Yeah, do need to check in real quick, though, Gary. I know you're busy. Do you have *any* interest in this?"

"In what?"

"In this. This relationship. This family. Are you ever going to work on any of this again? I'm asking for a friend."

I studied the wallpaper. Maybe the conversation would just go away.

"Well?" she continued. There's a long silence. Then: "*Well?*"

Still staring at the wall, I said: "Drama? Really? At this hour? Are you kidding me right now? I mean, you know what I'm going through, trying to get my footing again at the store. Attacking me at one in the morning? This is the support? Attacks? When I'm exhausted and you know I can't deal with this?"

"Gary, you're not even *looking* at me. You *do* realize that—that we don't even make *eye contac*t anymore. This is exactly what I'm *talking* —"

I turn over real fast and she stops talking. I look her right in the eye, and then I hear myself say the same thing we both know I told the teacher right before I decked him: *"Go. Fuck. Yourself."*

After that, I jumped out of bed and stalked out of the bedroom— loud—to go sleep on the couch. From that moment on, and for way longer than I feel like admitting, it was every man for himself in our marriage.

The whole time we'd known each other, I'd never talked to Melissa like that. Never. Even so, that part had bothered me for maybe a hundredth of a second, if even that long. Want to know why? Because I was an addict. Addicts don't care about that shit.

And you know what else? The amazing part? Even that night, Melissa had no idea what was really going on. Even that night, after I crossed the line (she told me later), she thought I was just tired of navigating family life. She thought maybe I had met someone else.

I was an experienced addict, meaning I was good at covering my tracks. I had a lot more experience with this game than Melissa did.

She caught on eventually, though, because this game is one nobody—and I do mean *nobody*—ever really wins. And here comes the subtext again, the quiet part right out loud, the *reason* I am shining a spotlight on me being such an asshole, the *reason* I am putting you through this, putting myself through this, putting everybody through this by writing all this sick shit down and asking you to read it.

The big takeaway for all of us, me included: *Do not stop going to the fucking meetings.*

48. ON BELIEVING EVERYTHING YOU THINK

Like a lot of addicts, I made everything about me. Every day, I was like:

Well, I know this probably isn't ideal, but the thing is, I really can't go to work effectively without the coke and without the pills, because I won't be on my game. I won't be able to talk to people or connect with people the way I'm doing right now, and that's the most important part of my job: talking to people and connecting with people. I'm on stage all day long, so obviously I've got to keep on doing it the way I'm doing it.[53]

That sounded persuasive to me at the time, and if you know anyone who's an addict, I can pretty much guarantee you that they've sold themselves a load of bullshit that sounds, to them, just as persuasive and feels just as obvious—but in reality is just as fucking absurd as anything the Flat Earthers could come up with. If that addict you know were to pause for, I don't know, 30 seconds and write down what they're telling themselves, they wouldn't want to show what they'd written or read it out loud to anyone. Something deep inside of them, a little voice, would whisper: *You know what? That's stupid, what you just wrote.*

But addicts learn to tune out that little voice. They get good at tuning it out completely, pretending it doesn't exist—and at the same time, they are silently repeating whatever lunatic justification they've just made for themselves and their toxic, addictive behavior.

Take me. Before I fell off the ladder and messed up my thumb, I was completely fine. I was more than holding my own creatively, the store was a success, I was doing my job really, really well and I wasn't using coke or pills—at all. But now that I *was* using, I had somehow convinced myself that I couldn't possibly do my job without cocaine and Oxycontin.

Addiction edits reason out of the addict's mind. This is why addicts need constant, ongoing, person-to-person contact with *other* addicts who are in recovery. We need to hear other people calling bullshit on the lies we feed ourselves, the lies that everyone in the room—except us—can instantly see are lies. Otherwise we believe everything we think, even when what we think is out to kill us.

We've got issues.

***

So, here's what happened as things fell down around me. My ego went on a bender.

Technically, The Comic Outpost may have been a retail outlet, but on an emotional level—which is what matters, because humans are, let's face it, emotional beings—the store was now a life support mechanism for my ego.

It's probably impossible to find the right words to convey exactly what it was like to be a traumatized nerd who happened to run a popular San Francisco comic store, and who also happened to spend large chunks of his day high on a cocktail of cocaine and Oxycontin and Vicodin

It's probably impossible to find words that will get across, to someone who was sane enough not to choose that path, just what choosing that path, day after toxic, self-medicated day, can do to your ego. Words can't possibly capture the sudden sense of being immortal, of being all-powerful, of being right about everything after all. And English will probably never be able to convey the rush that can send your ego soaring toward the mesosphere for those few, brief, mindblowing moments before fear and loathing, your old buddies, take control of the trip once again and suspend you, weightless, in the coldest corner of space—and then reverse your trajectory by restoring the law of gravity, driving you head-first down, down, down, faster and faster, toward what you sense in your gut can only be the deep, molten fucking core of Mother Earth (who is now pissed at you for imagining you could ever leave).

But goddammit, let's give words a try anyway. Here goes:

We've got issues.

I really, really, really don't want to glamorize this chapter of my life. I do have a responsibility to let you know, though, *why* my ego kept insisting that it knew exactly what it was doing. *Why* it kept begging me not to change course or even think about changing course, even when I could see the cliff I was approaching. *Why* my ego had programmed itself to keep playing tricks on me that would keep me coming back to a lifestyle that was clearly out to kill me. I have that responsibility because you or someone you know may end up having a similar conversation with an overblown ego just like mine.

You or someone you know may wake up to find an ego in the middle of a bender, right behind the wheel of a large automobile you happen to be in. And when that happens, there is no sense, none, in listening to what the ego has to say about the trip. The car has *got* to pull over. Safely. Fast. Period.

I am about to explain why my ego was running a number on me, so you can recognize the moment when your own overblown ego or someone else's is running a number on *you*—and driving you right toward a cliff.

Here's what that experience looked like for me.

Hundreds of people trusted me to know exactly what kinds of stories they liked, trusted me to make sure they got those stories on a regular basis. Hundreds of people hung out in the store because they liked reading the stories I pointed them toward. Hundreds of people sent their friends my way so I could point *those* friends toward stories *they* liked. My store was like a little city, a city made up of people who trusted me to tell them which story would be perfect for them. And I really got off on being the mayor of that little city. I loved it—and that was my ego's entry point.

My ego talked me into believing that I had to do exactly what it wanted if I wanted to be a good mayor and keep being a good mayor. And in that moment, I chose, against all the available evidence, to believe that my ego knew what it was doing.

So, when I heard my ego begging me for a direct hit of something in a glass vial, I saw myself hand over the vial. Then, I watched my ego drain that vial, heard it snort and howl and sprout claws and fangs and turn into a fucking werewolf and bellow to the full moon for more of it.

I saw my ego deciding it was a rock star, and I handed it the room keys. I watched it head upstairs. I saw it tossing the nearest television set out the nearest hotel window, and I watched that television land right in the center of the metaphorical swimming pool. The splash was amazing.

I heard my ego whispering to me that I was a dealer—the best kind of dealer imaginable, the one dealer that no one can possibly do without. I was the guy who supplied the stuff everyone on Planet Earth wants, 24/7: *joy*. Which meant I could get away with anything. Forever.

I bought all that bullshit my ego fed me. I bought it for two straight years.

For two years, I burned my way through all available cash. When it was gone, I started selling shit to pay for my habit. I snorted up everything I could get my hands on to sell, and I washed it all down with a chaser of Oxycontin and Vicodin.

***

When I think of all the stuff I sold so I could keep on doing coke, it breaks my fucking heart.

To be able to keep doing coke, I sold a John Byrne piece—a commissioned drawing Byrne did for me personally. This was a picture of Spider-Man and Batman on a double date with Catwoman and Black Cat, up on a rooftop. A beautiful piece, a one-of-a-kind piece.

The top left panel of the comic below has a drawing of it, but I don't have that piece anymore. I snorted it. I snorted everything. And when I looked up, a decade of my life was gone. It turned out I really had picked the right slogan for The Comic Outpost:

We've got issues.

In 10 years, I went from clean and sober and losing money on something I loved…

…to breaking even on something I loved…

…to finally being profitable doing something I loved…

…to relapsing and being an addict all over again.

WHAT I HAVE SOLD...

MELISSA EVENTUALLY
FIGURED IT OUT.

SHE HAD A LITTLE
SURPRISE IN STORE FOR ME.

CAN YOU SAY...
INTERVENTION?

PART FIVE: THWWIP!

In Part Five, there's an intervention. And some bumps in the road on the way back to sobriety. We learn how Melissa dealt with those bumps in the road, how I did, and what it took to get me back to "one day at a time." Also, I fixate on pop culture...and launch a podcast that eventually turns into a YouTube channel.

49. THE DEATH RAY

For a while now, Melissa had gotten all kinds of proof that the guy she'd trusted—and married—was an ever-more-distant, ever-more-aggressive, ever-less-supportive asshole. Now, one of the beautiful things about Melissa is that her default position is usually to assume the best about people. For a long time, much longer than I deserved, she'd assumed the best about me. There was a big stretch of time when she'd convinced herself that my "asshole phase" would eventually pass. I'd stop being so impossible to live with when my thumb had healed fully, when I'd gotten my footing back at The Comic Outpost, when [insert outside event here] happened.

But a day came when she couldn't keep on pretending I was going to get my footing back—not on my own, anyway. A day came when it was no longer possible to give me the benefit of the doubt, when it was obvious this wasn't about any outside event. A day came when Melissa connected the dots and decided, correctly, that this was all about Gary.

She was snooping around my home office—her suspicions had finally gotten the better of her—and she found clear signs that I was using drugs at home. Remember how I said I was really good at covering my tracks? Well, there comes a point where addicts are no longer so great at hiding stuff... or maybe they just care a whole lot less. In my case, it was a combination of the two.

The point here is: it became impossible for her not to connect the dots. She called me out.

She called me on it. We fought. I deflected. We fought some more. I deflected some more. As I deflected, I pushed her buttons, I got her enraged and I pretended that the real problem we were looking at as a couple was how angry she was when she communicated with me. Did she have a right to be angry? Did she have a reason to feel anger? Those really were not the issues I wanted to talk about; addressing them would have gotten in the way of me deflecting. Deflecting was what I was good at.

The point is, Melissa confronted me, I pushed back and we got nowhere. Nothing changed. Except our relationship became more toxic.

So, she decided it was time to take action—time to shake up our toxic status quo. She drew the line. And today, looking back, there are no words that can get across just how much I owe her for deciding to shake things up after connecting the dots and calling me on my bullshit. If Melissa hadn't taken action then, I don't think I'd be here to talk to you about everything that happened during that final year I owned The Comic Outpost.

I'd be too busy being dead.

Whenever Spider-Man finds himself in a tough spot during a fight with a super-villain, he has this cool trick he does. He keeps his pinky and index fingers extended outward, and pulls his ring and middle fingers inward so they press his lower palm.

When he does that, a jet of super-strong, hyper-flexible webbing shoots out from Spidey's inner wrist, and as it does so, it makes a cool sound effect, one that has become synonymous with Spider-Man himself: *THWWHIP!* The jet of webbing hurtles upward, attaches itself securely to a lamppost or a power pole or some other tall object, and becomes Spidey's means of escape from whatever deadly thing is careening toward him: fireball, death ray, you name it.

Whenever *THWWIP!* dominated a panel of a Spider-Man comic, you knew he was about to swing free from whatever that supervillain imagined was about to kill him. *THWWIP!* was Spidey getting out of trouble.

I thought I could count on my own *THWWIP!* factor indefinitely. I thought I'd always find a way to swing away from danger at the very last minute. If Melissa had never called me out, never drawn the line, I would have kept pressing my ring and middle fingers into my palm over and over again, but I never would have gotten out of the way of that deadly incoming death ray. I was facing a supervillain who overmatched me: addiction.

I was all out of *THWWIP!* She knew that, but I didn't. Maybe I could've called this book *How Gary Got His THWWIP! Back.*

Anyway, the point is: I could never have gotten it back without her.

50. BAD CRAZINESS

After one of our big arguments, I decided to make a trip down to San Diego for the Comic-Con that was happening down there. Honestly, my memory of this period of my life is still a little hazy, but I'm pretty sure the objective was to sell some stuff from my collection, generate some quick cash and use that cash to maintain my King Kong-sized cocaine habit that was riding hard on my back literally everywhere I went.

That was what was motivating me now: keeping that cocaine supply steady. In my twisted mind, cocaine was now synonymous with life support. I was really on a roll.

Anyway, I was on I-5 with my life-support mission accomplished (in the short term, anyway) and making my way back to San Francisco coked out, jumpy and strung out from too many long hours on the road, gripping my steering wheel with white knuckles. As I drove, the weirdest thing started jumping out at me: every other car I passed looked to me like it had to be an unmarked cop car.

I knew maybe not every other one was—but, you know, by the same token, why the fuck were so many Chevy Tahoes and Dodge Chargers all suddenly following me now?

What the hell was going on?

Okay, most important thing—keep all the options open, I thought. *Don't make this any worse*. It was possible that this was just bad craziness, chemically enhanced sleep deprivation playing tricks on me.

But possibly not.

I pulled out my phone and called Melissa—not to tell her about this latest problem, which obviously she wouldn't be able to handle or even comprehend, but just to let her know I'd be home soon. Mostly, what I needed her to understand was what I needed to do the very fucking moment I arrived home: collapse in my bed without any drama, with an emphasis on the "no drama" part. I needed sleep, and I needed rest—maybe the whole next day. That was not up for discussion. Did she understand all that?

There was this weird little pause before Melissa said, "Yes."

She was waiting for me to hang up. I thought I had, but apparently I hadn't, because a couple of minutes later, the phone startled the shit out of me when it said, in Melissa's voice:

"Gary?"

I hit the red phone icon and the call was over. I hadn't slept in at least the past 36 hours.

I was maybe an hour and a half away from home—less if I found a way to make up some time. Ninety more minutes was all I had to manage without incident. The highway rolled out ahead of me, dark and stripe-lined and way, way too straight. White line fever, the truckers called it. I rolled down the window so the breeze could help keep me awake. The wind rushed in and I checked the rear-view mirror.

Shit. Chevy Tahoe alert.

There it was again, dammit, yet another undercover vehicle—another car that looked like a fucking undercover vehicle, anyway—and it was trying to pass me. It was some sort of coordinated roadblock operation, obviously, the motherfuckers.

"Yeah? You sure?" I said to myself. "You wanna gun it, Pops?"

I put my right foot down, daring the bastards, all of them, to put their cards on the goddamned table for once and try to pull me over.

"Just try it. See what happens."

The old guy in the car that had been trying to pass me eased off. Clearly, I'd made my point.

"That's what I'm saying!" I shouted to all the would-be undercover cops in the universe. "Don't do it. Don't fuck with me. I'm a citizen. I have rights." I kept up the pressure on the gas pedal.

"That's better, assholes. Back off."

The stripes and the lightposts started hurtling past me, faster and faster. They started to blur. Hmm…they didn't usually do that, did they? Blur together? I hadn't checked the speedometer recently and I wondered what it said. Might be interesting to find out.

A quick glance at my dashboard told me I was doing 105. It occurred to me that maybe, just maybe, I might have wandered outside of my goddamned mind.

I took the deepest breath I could manage, then slowed, ever so gradually, ever so purposefully, to 65. I checked my trajectory, my left and right windows and my rear-view mirror. Apparently, I hadn't killed anyone. I saw the exit for 580 approaching, and I signaled, merged with great care and took it.

Somehow, don't ask me how, no flashing lights lit up in my rear-view mirror the whole way home.

51. THIS IS NOT A PARTY

Now, I didn't know this at the time, but Melissa was already thinking about what to do next. She was following a bulletproof, three-part plan. Her logic, which was unassailable, and it looked like this:

1. It was time for Gary to go into rehab. That's what needed to happen next.

2. She couldn't do that part on her own. The rehab place was two hours away. Gary would spend the whole drive trying to worm his way out of getting help, therefore:

3. If Gary made it back from San Diego, she was going to need some help getting him there.

Note the *if* in that last part. I was posting some pretty crazy shit on my socials from Comic-Con. Like I said, my memory of this phase is a little hit-or-miss, but Melissa remembers thinking that it was not at all a sure thing that I would make it home in one piece (or make it home at all). That gives you a sense of where I'd left my family life, and where my priorities were at this stage.

Anyway, Melissa's idea was that, assuming I was still alive and capable of making it home and walking in the door, an intervention would be waiting for me. She'd taken all our remaining savings—the little money she'd been able to firewall so she could be sure I wouldn't snort it—and she'd used it to pay for the rehab and to hire the intervention guy.

That was what I walked in on, visibly worse for wear and tear, exhausted, and coked out of my head. I remember noticing there were more people than usual in the house, which was something I hadn't expected. I thought that a party must've been going on.

In the living room, I saw Jim, a buddy of Melissa's I'd known for a while. Jim was someone I remembered liking a lot and hanging out with back in the days when I was going to meetings. Lately, I had been avoiding his company, for obvious reasons—but Jim was the kind of guy I'd respected for years but hadn't seen in a while. He'd been sober for a long time. He had a lot of miles in on his own recovery. But the fact that Jim was there didn't clue me in to what I was looking at. *Wow, Jim's come over for a party!* I thought. *That's cool. Maybe I'll hang out with Jim for a few minutes before I head to bed.*

There was this dude standing next to Jim that I didn't recognize, and there was Melissa, of course. All three of them were staring at me, and I was still clueless. I made my way into the living room and said, "Hey guys, what's up?"

Melissa didn't say anything, which was the first thing that seemed a little strange to me. The silence didn't last long. Jim took the lead.

"Hey, Gary, come on in and have a seat," he said, gesturing to an open chair. "We really need to talk to you about something serious."

Just from the tone in Jim's voice, a little switch in my head clicked. Suddenly, I knew what this was.

Now, I was thinking: *Ah. This is not a party. This is an intervention. Okay. Decision time. What do I do?*

The answer that came back, and I mean *instantly* came back, was: *Man, I just want this to be over.*

I was ready to get off the crazy ride I was on, no matter what it took, and this was an opportunity to get off. Didn't even think about it, didn't even question it. *Fine, intervene. Sure. Let's go.*

Looking back, I realize this was kind of like the moment when I got busted: Okay, well, looks like this is serious. I had no illusions about what was going on. There was no part of me trying to figure out how I could get out of it. Leaving the house and getting back in that car, or pursuing any other avenue of escape, seemed like way, way too much effort. Why not just do it? Why not just get it the fuck over with?

I sat down right where Jim was pointing. Half an hour later, I was agreeing to get into a car with the guy I hadn't recognized when I came into the house.

As he guided me, wobbly, toward the door, Melissa said, "Try and have a good time."

52. DRY DRUNK

In August of 2013, I reported to rehab at this place Melissa had found for me in Scotts Valley. We told the kids I was going to summer camp, which was true, I guess. It was summer, and it was a camp. There was a major outdoor vibe to the place. I guess the idea was that communing with nature was supposed to have some sort of healing effect.

I did what I was supposed to do. I started doing meetings again, because you have to, in that environment. And yes, I got clean and came home. Melissa, who had started going to Al-Anon by this point, decided, provisionally, to let me back in the house. This all happened pretty fast, within three months or so.

But when I went back to work, I relapsed again.

I started lying and covering up (again). I kept Melissa out of the loop (again). I used button-pushing to set off some really dysfunctional conflict cycles (again), all so I could use coke (again). Running a comic store was still a great way to run into people who are happy to offer you drugs. And I still had—you guessed it—issues.

To all the addicts and alcoholics reading this, there's something important I need to share before we go any further about those places that give you a month or two of so-called "intense" rehab, operating on the idea that a month or two is enough to turn your life around for good and keep it turned around.

Here's the part I want to make sure I get into this book: sometimes people do have that positive experience with these places. A lot of times, though, they don't.

Way too often, they go through what I went through: immersion (or, in my case, re-immersion) with the basic principles of recovery and enough peer reinforcement to get them to the point where they really do stop using or drinking—but there's still an unsolved problem. Whatever trauma happened, whatever unaddressed crap made them an addict in the first place, *remains* unaddressed and undealt with. And they still don't realize it. They don't know how fucked up they are inside. Not yet.

So: You do your month. You get a sponsor. You start working the steps. You're not drinking. You're not using. *But you've still got issues.*

You're vulnerable. Summer camp or no summer camp, you're not in a position where you can protect yourself yet. Believe me, because I speak from experience. That's exactly where I was after summer camp: incapable of protecting myself. But the thing is, being sober is not the end game. It's not even close to the end game. There *is* no end game. Recovery is a lifetime gig.

You really *can* be sober without fully understanding, or even beginning to understand, the stuff that drove you to become an addict in the first place. You *can* be sober without even identifying, much less working on, the brokenness that led you to self-medicate. It's called being a dry drunk, and that's where I was when I got out of Folsom. That's where I was 17 years later, when I relapsed the first time after I fucked up my thumb. And that's where I was when I got out of Scotts Valley and relapsed again. I was a dry drunk—or, in my case, a dry addict, I guess.

The tricky thing about being a dry drunk is you think you've already hit bottom. I am here to tell you that sometimes you might *imagine* you've hit bottom, but there's actually a whole new level of bottom just biding its time, waiting for you. Please, please understand: that new level of bottom is out there in the parking lot, doing pushups.

It's getting stronger every day, just waiting for you to slip up.

So do the goddamned work.

53. NOT DOING THE WORK

To get back to our story, I was using again—heavily. I was imagining I was doing a great job of hiding my coke habit from everyone in my life, but even though I'd managed to persuade Melissa that I was still in recovery somehow, and even though no one at the store was willing to call me out on my behavior, the reality was that The Comic Outpost was cratering. It was cratering in that fascinating, entertaining way that enterprises run by drug addicts always crater: by destroying important relationships left and right.

At the time, I may have told myself I was now some kind of expert when it came to concealing a major coke habit, but deep down, there was a part of me that knew it was unsustainable. I was burning through cash again, and I was treating people like crap again. Neither of those things stay secret for long.

People would ask me how my life was now that I'd "been through rehab."

"It's cool, I'm fine," I'd respond. "In fact, it's time to go to a meeting."

Then, I would go to a meeting and do my best to bullshit my way through it, but it was obvious that I just wasn't doing the work. That's about all I was good at during this phase: not doing the work.

It got to a point where I was *pretending* to go to meetings: taking off for an hour, coming back and acting like everything was great before snorting my way down the highway. Life in the fast lane, right? I had multiple sponsors who later showed up in person to fire me for not returning phone calls. Those were some fun conversations.

It was really, really, really bad, and I knew how bad it was, too.

I knew this was way worse than when I was that confused kid doing a bunch of drugs just because I was a confused kid doing a bunch of drugs. Now, it was different. Now, I had a wife and two kids to take care of and employees who were all counting on me, and I was sitting in the shadows, wiping my nose, shuddering, opening the door, screaming at people and living an absolute lie.

Eventually, it all came crashing down. I went through a very public relapse, my second relapse in just about eight weeks. Bottom line: I did a whole lot of damage in a remarkably short timespan, and a lot of people got front-row seats for that show, starting with my wife and my employees. Those poor employees had to go through a lot of shit, more than I have time or space to tell you about here. Suffice to say the financial position of the store suffered exactly the way you'd expect it to if a cokehead was running the circus, and I had a bunch of new amends to make. I victimized a lot of people, and I put a lot of people through the wringer.

Eventually, I had to admit that me owning the store was over. It wasn't good for my recovery, and I knew I couldn't recover financially. The Comic Outpost was now in a death spiral, and I wasn't in a position to pull it out. I wanted to close it, just so I could get some closure for myself.

I didn't get that clean break, though, because another shop owner put an offer in on my store. By this point, The Comic Outpost had 500-plus subscribers, a building and a big inventory of books and merch, so even though I had snorted up all the operating capital, the store was still worth something. While closing the shop might have been attractive in theory, I had the customers and a family to consider. We needed the money. So I took the offer.

It was the equivalent of fumbling the ball in a dash toward the endzone and watching as someone from the other team scooped up the ball, headed in the opposite direction and scored the winning touchdown. Watching that ball move down the field in someone else's hands was just gut-wrenching.

That particular game, though, was over. All over.

54. THE MELISSA METHOD

Remember how, while I was away at summer camp, Melissa started going to Al-Anon?

There's easily a whole book's worth of material we could cover about the support she got there, the critical lessons she learned about recovery and the way-too-easy-to-overlook fact that addiction/alcoholism is a family disease. I do wish there was space here to share all of that with you, but there's not. So, I'll do the next best thing.

I'll cue up this next little interaction by reminding everyone reading this who loves an addict/alcoholic, living or dead, of two things. Melissa keeps bugging me about these two things, keeps asking me about them, keeps checking whether they're in the book yet.

Dear Everyone Who Loves an Addict/Alcoholic:

First, you are not alone.

And second, the sooner you take advantage of the love, support and accumulated tribal wisdom that's waiting for you at Al-Anon, the healthier and happier you will be.

(Now they're in the book—moving on.)

Interesting scenario: suppose you found yourself in Melissa's position. Suppose you woke up one morning and realized you were married to someone with a long, complex, painful and traumatic personal history, someone who had a major drug addiction that was about to do him in.

And suppose that spouse of yours had relapsed not once but twice in a 60-day timeframe. Suppose you had figured all of that out. Suppose you'd seen through all the lies. And suppose you loved this person—but you also loved your two kids, and you just flat-out weren't willing to bring them up in an environment where Dad is using *lots* of drugs *all the fucking time*.

What would you do?

Well, here's one possible way to address that situation. It's based on what Melissa did when she was facing just such a problem. We'll call it the Melissa Method.[54]

First, do some on-line research about "sober living environments"—that's the phrase for Google. Find a few you feel good about that are close enough for you to drive to. Make some calls. Audition these places. Consider them job applicants. Remember, you're choosing whether *you* feel comfortable working with *them*, not the other way around.

Next, wait till your addict husband is out of the house for one of those mysterious, unexplained two-day-long absences of his. You'll notice this time has begun because the house will feel more peaceful and calm—not just for a few minutes, but for an extended period of time. You will feel less like you're walking on eggshells, less like you need to protect yourself and your kids from something that's about to explode for no identifiable reason. You'll feel less anxious. You'll notice yourself taking more deep breaths. You'll find yourself hoping this peaceful feeling lasts. Once you notice that hope, *use the time you've been given*.

Arrange for someone you trust to watch the kids. Get them out of the house if at all possible. Make it possible.

Next, *take this opportunity to pack up all your addict husband's essential shit* while he's not around (yep, just like his ex-wife did, back in the day). Put everything he's going to need for the next week or so into suitcases, boxes, plastic bags, whatever. You can drop off more stuff later as needed. Pack light, but pack in such a way as to eliminate possible debates and excuses when he shows up, figures out what's going on and starts looking for reasons to deflect, change the subject, explode, whatever.

Put all that stuff in your vehicle—presumably he's using the other one for only God-knows-what. Make sure there is gas in that vehicle. Make sure that vehicle is in good repair.

Give yourself some kind of appropriate calming reward once everything has been packed and put in the car. Use whatever time is still left before he returns to your orbit to be good to yourself. Relax, restore and recharge. You will need all the energy and all the resilience you can muster for what comes next.

When your addict husband shows up again at your house, looking like hell as usual, spoiling for a fight as usual, *turn on the charm machine.* Be all happy and upbeat. Do not respond to any attacks he may launch. Do not acknowledge the existence of any attacks he may launch. Do not let him push your buttons. Do not engage in any way with any bullshit, period. Just keep running what we're going to call the Charm Machine. Smile your best 1000-watt smile and talk, talk, talk.

As you run the Charm Machine at full throttle, make a point of saying happy, happy, happy things and staying in constant motion. Bounce around the room optimistically. The idea is to act like you're about to embark on a major adventure together (you are). No matter what he says or doesn't say, keep the Smile Machine running and use positivity to control the narrative. You have a right to control the narrative.

With the Charm Machine going at full blast, start saying things like: *"Guess what? Great news! You are not going to believe how lucky we are! We've caught a major break!"* If possible, keep him from speaking at all. Start monologuing. Just focus nonstop on the wonderfulness of it all. The luckiness of it all. The amazing, totally unexpected, coming-togetherness of it all. He's likely to be caught off guard and confused by this—which of course was your desired outcome. At some point, he'll say something like, "Lucky? What do you mean, lucky? What are you talking about?"

Act surprised. Look at him funny. Act like you've been talking about this for months (you haven't, of course, but act like you have.) Resume the 1000-watt smile and explain, patiently, but without relinquishing control of the topic, that *of course* you're talking about the sober living environment he's going to stay in.

Then say, "It's time to get in the car. Let's go."

Be prepared for him to look you in the eye and go, "WHOA. Whoa, hold on."

Then and only then, *turn off the Charm Machine*. Turn off the happy talk. Look him straight in the eye. Let him know you mean what you're about to say.

As you maintain intense eye contact with your addict husband, say, **"No, there's no WHOA. I'm not letting you stay here anymore. Get in the fucking car."**

Mean that shit. Walk his ass out to the fucking car. Get him buckled in. Get behind the wheel. Get yourself bucked in. Start the car. Drive, safely and carefully, to the sober living environment. Obey all traffic regulations en route. Do not speak to your addict husband. Do not respond to any remark, complaint or threat you hear. Keep driving safely. Focus on the road ahead.

Once you get to the sober living environment, drop his ass off on the curb. Tell him to get his own goddamned bags out of the car.

IMPORTANT: Before he closes the car door or trunk, he will try to talk to you. *Do not let him.*

Say, "Close the fucking door," or, "Close the fucking trunk." Whichever is appropriate to the situation.

Once he does that, and you are positive you're not going to hit him, gun the engine (loud), put the car in gear, hit the accelerator and burn rubber. Get the hell out of there. You will know you've done this properly if you can both hear the rear wheels screech as you drive away. It's very, very important that he hears the wheels screech. Once he hears those wheels screech, he will know he's hit bottom.

That's the Melissa Method.

It worked for us.

55. THE SLE DISCLAIMER

The big danger here is that people may read this next part and come away with the idea that sober living environments (SLEs)—which are basically residential spaces that give addicts/alcoholics a supportive, highly structured, substance-free place to do the hard personal work of recovery—are what "really work" when your life is falling apart. What I mean is that addicts, alcoholics and those who love them may read this next part and decide, based on what happened to me, that an SLE is "the answer" for them just because I've built a story around it.

I know stories can be powerful, especially when you're looking for answers in your life. I know they're important. But I need to put a disclaimer here before we continue this particular story.

Yes, I saved my life and got my family back after I spent a lot of time (and money) in an SLE. Yes, it's time to tell you about that now. And yes, we're getting close to the end of the book. So that must be the takeaway of this whole thing, right?

I mean, doesn't the problem get *solved*, for good? What kind of story is it if the problem *isn't* solved for good once the book ends? *Aren't* SLEs the answer? If not, what is?

Those are, and I say this with all respect, all the wrong questions to ask.

I know there are plenty of great reasons for asking questions like that, but hear me out: I've been down this road. I have two big reasons for asking a different question: *How ready are you to commit to the work?*

First, and probably most important, let's understand that the whole recovery movement is built on the principle that there is no definitive, permanent "answer" to addiction and alcoholism. We never, ever get to tell ourselves that we've solved this problem. That's important to know going in. Imagining you've finally solved it is hubris, and hubris equals relapse.

So let me be brutally honest and clear with you about this: I am an addict right now. That's not humble AA talk. That's a fact. I'm an addict, I'm in recovery and as this book goes to press, my recovery seems to be going pretty well. I'm grateful for that. But I'm not counting my chickens. I'm not taking anything for granted about what will or won't happen in the future. All I've got is today, and today, I'm an addict who's still recovering.

That fact has not gone away from my life. It's not going to go away. That's just how this works. One way or another, I will be an addict until the day I die.

Here it comes again. Yes, I am putting this in the book twice—that's how important this is:

> **"We are not cured of alcoholism (or addiction). What we really have is a daily reprieve contingent on the maintenance of our spiritual condition."**
> **–The Big Book**

Okay, having said that, the second big reason there's no one-size-fits all solution that I can point you toward, or that anyone can point you toward, is this:

Your level of personal commitment to this work has a way of depending on whether you've hit rock bottom.

If you haven't hit rock bottom, you may not be willing—yet—to hold yourself accountable for addressing your own brokenness, one day at a time, forever.

It's a lot of work, and it never ends. If you're not personally committed to it, it doesn't happen.

No, I'm not telling you to go out and get drunk, snort coke, take pills and rocket your way toward disaster. *What I'm telling you is that holding yourself accountable is the only place healing starts.* If you're not there yet, you're vulnerable—no matter what program you're in.

56. ROCK BOTTOM

Standing there on the sidewalk, hearing those tires squeal and watching Melissa's car disappear, I knew I'd finally hit rock bottom. This was, no bullshit, the part of the story where my life had to change. That was non-negotiable. I had to get my family back. Whatever it took to make that happen, I was ready to do.

The first decision I had to make was probably the toughest one. Getting my family back started with accepting the reality that my wife had just told me to get the fuck out of the house and out of her life—and stay out until I was clean and sober.

That woman, the woman I loved, had just driven away loud enough for me and the whole world to hear what she was saying: Protecting herself and protecting her kids was more important than knowing what was going to happen to me.

My first decision was accepting her right to do that.

Melissa had chosen to control the only thing she could: whether there was an addict under her roof. Fighting that choice, I now saw, was pointless. I had no right to assume she would ever agree to talk to Addict Gary again. If I was using, I was out of her life, and out of our kids' lives. Period. That was where me being a drug addict had brought us as a family.

That was my starting point. If I didn't respect her decision, if I called her and tried to prove how right I was about something, if I made any attempt to make my way back into her life without getting clean first, it would be all over between us. For good. There would be no coming back from that.

I picked up my stuff from the curb, carried it all over to the front door, set it down on the stoop and rang the bell.

57. THE BALANCE SHIFTS

About half an hour later, the little guy with the squeaky voice who ran the place—I guess—stood me up, took my arm and walked me out of the living room. That's where I'd been waiting, getting ready for the next piece of crap news the universe was getting ready to drop-kick into my face.

As he walked, Squeaky Voice said he needed to talk to me about something. Based on the direction he was pointing as we walked, the speed of his step and the fact that it looked like he was now *only* willing to talk to me at a fair distance from the other residents, I had a pretty good idea what the little guy wanted to discuss.

"You failed your pee test," he said. "You can't stay here tonight. Your bags are in the hall. Come back tomorrow and you can take the test again. If you pass tomorrow, you can stay."

Crap news. Right in my face.

What Melissa hadn't taken into account on that icy, silent trip over to the SLE was that, to enter a sober living environment, you have to be sober. And I had been ingesting way more than my fair share of cocaine for the past...let's just say for a while.

"Yeah," I said, my chest suddenly tense and rigid, "but where am I supposed to *go?*"

The way Squeaky Voice shrugged before he opened the front door gave me the sense he'd heard that question before. He also seemed to know I wouldn't be staying with Melissa tonight, and that I didn't have the money for even a cheap hotel room.[55]

"Maybe your car?" he said. "Up to you, really."

"Are you *shitting* me? We're *paying* you for this place and you're sending me out onto the *street?* Do you have any *idea* what I've been through today?"

The little guy locked eyes with me and said—very quietly and calmly, but still very squeaky: "Every time we complain about something external, we're giving up our power in our own life. We're saying that we want someone else to make decisions for us. I don't get the sense that you're that kind of guy."

I had absolutely no comeback for that.

"Now, if you want, Gary," he went on, "I can call you a cab, but you'll need to be able to pay for it, and I'll want to see the money before I make the call."

The tone of this guy's voice was really beginning to grate on me. I picked up my bags.

"It's okay," I said. "I'll walk. Maybe you could call Melissa and let her know I'm coming back just to get my car—so I can bring it back here and park it out front. Tell her I won't try to go into the house. Make sure she knows, okay?"

He nodded. I left. He closed the door behind me.

I spent that night in my car. It sucked.

The next morning, the little guy came out front and knocked on my window. Hard. He seemed to enjoy waking me up.

He motioned, way too enthusiastically, for me to unroll the window, which I did. Then, he told me there was another SLE that would let me stay there, even if I failed the pee test. He gave me directions.

I rolled the window back up and started the car.

Just as well. That guy had been getting on my nerves.

58. WAITING FOR GARY

I did 90 meetings over the first 90 days at that other SLE, the SLE without the squeaky-voiced guy who annoyed me but who nailed it on the whole complaining thing. I never saw that guy again, that irritating guy who somehow got me on the exact right trajectory at the precise moment I needed, with precisely the words I needed to hear to make the next 90 days connect so I could get my shit together, do the work, get sober and get ready to make my case to Melissa. And Melissa was, I had to assume, pretty tired by now of waiting for Gary to get his shit together.

I couldn't blame her. She'd been waiting for Gary to get his shit together for a long, long time—longer than Gary wanted to admit. And I do mean *way* longer.

Why would I want to remind myself of all those times I'd promised I would call back—back when we were teenagers I mean—and never did? Why would I want to acknowledge all those hours she spent waiting for the phone to ring years ago, decades ago now, waiting for even a shred of evidence that I was something other than the world's worst boyfriend?

Now, she was waiting for the phone to ring all over again. Waiting for even a shred of evidence that I was something other than the world's worst husband. The world's worst father.

Waiting for Nerdrotic. To do the fucking work.

I realize 90 meetings in 90 days sounds like a lot of meetings, and maybe it is. But I hope you've picked up by now that just being in attendance at that many meetings doesn't mean you're no longer an addict. You've got to do the fucking work. More than that, you've also got to make sure you get the support you need while you're doing the work. Because no one, and I do mean no one, does this alone.

I knew Melissa was not willing or able to give me the support I needed at that moment. And I, obviously, wasn't in a position to give her a lot of support, either—remember, she was going to Al-Anon.

Other people, fortunately for both of us, *were* in a position to help each of us.

Recovery is an unpredictable process. You get these incredibly important life lessons from people who might otherwise qualify, at least at first, as total strangers (Squeaky Voice, for instance). Sometimes you never see them again, but you can't really call them strangers anymore, because they played a massive role in you doing the work you needed to do to reclaim your own life.

I don't know what to call these people. I mention them, though, so you can stay on the lookout for them. Because I promise you: they're out there, waiting for you. And once they give you something you need, you've got a job to do: help someone else out who needs to get on the right trajectory. Pay it back. Maybe not today, maybe not tomorrow—you'll know when it's your turn. But once you know it is, I want you to pay it back. Do that without ego. Do it without expecting anything in return. Do it without expecting to ever see them again. But do it, okay?

We're getting close to the end here, and there's still this nagging feeling that I have not quite gotten across how serious this shit was to me as I drove the three or four long miles to the address Squeaky Voice had just given me. So please, let me spend just a minute or two on how dialed in I was at that moment on doing the work, because that's how dialed in you have to be to get clean.

This was life or death. I knew that now. It had really taken me 20 years for that to sink in, for me to truly understand that much. Prior to my two—count 'em, two—relapses in three months, I had 17 years sober, but I really hadn't grasped that my life was what was at stake. If I wanted to be a dad and a husband again—and I did, because I knew my wife and kids had already been let down enough—then I had to totally commit myself once I got to this fucking SLE. If I went back to being an addict just one more time, I would be dead. And I didn't want to be dead.

I had zero room for error. I couldn't repeat any mistakes. So I knew I had to commit fully to this. And commitment, as it turns out, was the single biggest takeaway that I got from my time in the SLE.

59. COMMITMENT IS WHAT GETS YOU THROUGH

This takeaway came right at the top of the list of lessons that I knew I had to hold onto with both fucking hands—and that I am still holding onto, thank God, as I write this today. There were three big takeaways from the SLE, for me anyway, and this one was the first. It showed up at the very top of the priority list, before I even walked in the door. It was the one that got me through: *commitment.*

I don't know shit about tomorrow, but as I stand before you right now, today, I can say I am totally committed. I will not miss meetings, and I will do the work in those meetings. That's who I am. Right now, I do one meeting a week, non-negotiable. That started in SLE, with those 90 meetings over the first 90 days.[56]

Maybe you're wondering exactly how I made absolutely fucking certain I stayed committed to my own recovery during that time I spent in a sober living environment?

I'm so glad you asked.

What Gary Did in the SLE to Make Absolutely Fucking Sure He Stayed Committed to His Own Recovery

1. **I found a really, really great sponsor who understood how to interact with someone who has ADHD.** I have burned through a whole lot of sponsors in my day. When I went into the SLE, I knew I needed a sponsor relationship that would stick—not just any sponsor, but someone I had good rapport with, who understood me (and vice versa) and who was willing to navigate the difficult terrain that comes with accepting an addict with ADHD as a

sponsee. I found that person, and once I found him, I held onto that relationship for dear life. (Side note: To everyone out there sponsoring someone with ADHD or someone who you think *might* have ADHD—sometimes us not returning your calls really is us not being accountable to our commitments, but sometimes it's just us losing track of who we need to call back. Yes, there is some overlap between these two circles. We're not saying there's not. We're just asking you to remember that both circles exist.) Anyway: step one on deepening your commitment to your own recovery is having a sponsor who gets you and helps you feel good about making commitments.

2. **I took on the job of being Group Secretary at AA meetings.** There's healing in the act of contribution. There's healing in choosing to serve others. I needed to heal, so that's what I did— and who knows, contribution might work for you if you find yourself in a similar situation. Because if you're honest with yourself, which I highly recommend, you're probably going to reach a point in recovery where you admit that you really aren't all that happy with your progress, where you feel like you're not doing enough and not growing enough. You're going to feel like there's something missing. One great way to change that feeling is through *service*. Now, I was lucky—my sponsor knew this, and he knew me. He picked up on my restlessness, my need to do more than what I was doing, and he suggested that I take on the unpaid gig of Group Secretary for our meetings. The Group Secretary does a lot of stuff: makes the coffee, opens the doors to let people in, finds speakers for the next week. There's a whole list. It's a pretty big commitment, which, you'll recall, was what I really wanted to make. A big commitment. So, after that nudge from my sponsor, I went for it. I was all in. I figured, *Hey, this is all about commitments, so I'm making a commitment. I'm going to be the best fucking coffee maker in the history of AA meetings.* As a general rule, I'm not much of a fan of bragging on myself, but I will go out of

my way to take full credit for this one. I rocked the house. I will put my coffee-making, door-opening, speaker-finding record up against any Group Secretary for any meeting, anywhere. I *owned* that shit. That's how I had to approach it: that I was going to be the best there ever was at that job. That's what I had to do to find a way to get connected back to AA, because I knew that was the only place on the planet that was not going to judge me. Doing this work deepened my commitment to my own recovery—my commitment to working on myself.

3. **Working out.** I should say here that the SLE I spent time in was highly structured, but it wasn't like being in prison, because you could come and go as you pleased provided you agreed to abide by the house rules (which included regular drug tests). I mention this because it surprises some people to learn that during my time at the SLE, I rediscovered something that ended up being crucial to my personal commitment to recovery: getting out and going to the gym on a daily basis. This is one of the aspects of sobriety that people don't talk about enough: Work out! Get your heart pumping! No joke. Find a routine that's right for you, a routine that your doctor signs off on, then go for it. I worked out a lot while I was in Folsom, and I kept that up for a long time after I got out. It was a coping mechanism, yes, but it's important to remember that not all coping mechanisms are toxic (comic books, for instance—but I digress). You know what I noticed, looking back on my time being sober versus my time careening toward a relapse? There was a direct correlation between me not working out and me deciding I didn't have to go to meetings. *Hmm....*So, yes, it was while I was in the SLE that I decided to commit myself to hitting the gym daily—which, by the way, is still something I do today. I don't go to meetings every day anymore, but I sure as hell do work out every day (side benefit: I lost that flabby comic shop owner bod).

4. **I worked the 12 Steps like a motherfucker.** This point may seem basic, and today I'd agree that it certainly should be considered basic, but as a matter of history, it's been surprisingly easy for a lot of people in recovery (Addict Gary, for instance) to lose sight of. The point being, I made a personal commitment to *keep coming back* to the 12 Steps, even though I'd supposedly "worked my way through" all 12 of them before. Again, when it comes to recovery, we're never really "done" with these steps. *I* certainly wasn't done with them. I've said it before, but this is a lifelong journey. I got an important new perspective on this while I was in the sober living environment. Remember that new sponsor I found, the one I really clicked with? He made a point of emphasizing that he expected his sponsees to repeat the steps roughly *once a year*. Genius. Or basic common sense. Whichever it was, that approach has really helped me to deepen my personal commitment to my own recovery. Sometimes, people in recovery have this ongoing conversation: What's the hardest of the 12 steps? Personally, I think it's the fourth one—conducting a fearless personal inventory— because no matter how thoroughly you work on completing that step, and no matter how solid and well intentioned your effort is, a year later, you're going to know yourself better (if you don't, there's a problem somewhere.) And once you realize you know things about yourself that you didn't know before, your personal inventory is out of date. It needs revisiting. That's not just me. I'm going to go out on a limb here and say that goes for everyone in recovery.

Let's face it: we've got issues. And those issues are always going to challenge us to keep working on ourselves.

Which brings me to the second big takeaway I got from the sober living environment.

60. FORGIVENESS IS A SURVIVAL STRATEGY

This is the second big takeaway I got from the SLE. It's something I only figured out by re-engaging with the fourth of the 12 steps: **making a searching and fearless moral inventory of my own life.**

Remember what I told you about the "dry drunk"? The one who may not be using or drinking alcohol and maybe hasn't for years, but who still hasn't managed to identify or even address the brokenness that made self-medication a priority in the first place? That was me.

Want to know how I know? For 17 years, I was technically sober...but I was still having these detailed fantasies about slowly murdering the teacher who abused me when I was a kid.

I always snuffed him out in a dark basement, a place that let no light in from the outside world. I gave him just a puny, 50-watt bulb hanging from overhead so he could see what I was doing to him, but I kept the room dark enough for me to step back into the shadows whenever I wanted. I always made his death as agonizing and painful and bloody as I could. I just could not get enough of watching that guy die.

That shit is not healthy.

And the tricky part is you can know that *intellectually* and still be a dry drunk. You can know, intellectually, that you're supposed to say the words "I forgive him" out loud. And you can say those words and think you mean them. But you're still a dry drunk. How do you know? Again: Stuff like recurrent, dark fantasies of killing people. Big tipoff.

So, it was in SLE that I figured out that I had some work to do in terms of processing what had happened to me and how I felt about this guy. It was in SLE that I figured out that the reason I needed to focus on forgiveness was for me. Not for him, for me.

Honestly, for me, forgiveness—not just toward that guy in particular, but as a principle for getting through the day—is all about survival. It's about learning to be a better human, so that I can get better at processing traumatic experiences, working through them, being a healthier person and making healthier choices. For me, forgiveness is about surviving, then thriving.

Up to the point that I went into the SLE, I'd been making a whole lot of choices that were toxic and dangerous. I had to accept that me not having reached a point of forgiveness was part of that cycle. Just saying the words "I forgive so-and-so" and then continuing to envision their dismemberment in as much detail as possible on a regular basis was a flashing red light that I was choosing to ignore, a signal that I had work to do. Ignoring that work didn't help anyone, least of all me. It didn't make me a better husband, a better father, a better friend, a better anything. It made me worse at everything I did, and it made all my choices, in whatever role I took on, less likely to help me or the people I loved.

I'm not saying forgiveness should have happened overnight or could have happened overnight for me. What I'm saying is that it could probably have happened sooner than it did; that I was a better, healthier human being when it did happen and that I don't think it would have happened if I hadn't been committed to working the steps on an ongoing and totally committed basis (and particularly the fourth).

Two things are important to understand here. First, forgiveness is not reconciliation. You can forgive someone and not be willing or able to have an ongoing relationship with them, because the two of you haven't reconciled. You can forgive someone who is no longer part of your life for whatever reason: they're dead, they've got Alzheimer's, they're missing in action, whatever. You can forgive someone who has not changed their abusive, violent, destructive or otherwise unacceptable behavior cycles in any way. Forgiveness does not mean you approve of that person or endorse anything they did or didn't do. Forgiveness just means you let go (as some wise person once said) of all hope for a better past.

The second important thing to understand is that letting go of that hope for a better past isn't always easy. Just saying the words "I forgive you," doesn't magically make that letting-go happen. Why not? Because we're human beings. If something awful happens to us, we have to process it, and people process stuff in their own way. For most of us, talking it through in depth with someone who's willing to listen without judgment is how we speed up the process and get better, quicker. Once we get comfortable talking it out like I did in SLE, we can make our way to the next step—the step that makes it possible to let go, the step that reawakens empathy and gives us the ability to distance ourselves from the situation and assess it like a functioning, healing human being: Wow, something really fucked up must have happened to this guy. He was deeply broken as a human being.

That's the point I had to get to before I could forgive him: the point of empathy. The point of shared humanity. Don't misunderstand: I'd still cast a vote for him to go to jail. I still feel huge regret over the fact that he went on to do the same thing to other people. But I've forgiven him. I'm one human being choosing to let go of what happened with another human being. I had to talk those experiences through before I could let them go—but I let them go. They're not part of my identity anymore. I'm not stuck in that place of hatred anymore. There are many, many dark places like that for addicts, not just one place. Holding on to those places, and I do speak from personal experience on this, is poison. Staying in that kind of dark place fuels addiction. Standing in the shadows of that basement didn't *hurt* him. It hurt *me*.

It took me two times around to figure that out. You know, I could still hold on to this anger if I wanted to, but that would be wasting a lot of time and energy blaming how unfair my life was (or is) on someone else. That would mean me being in prison. And I am done with prison.

Maybe you've got anger like that, anger based on something that's happened in your past. Or maybe you're dealing with something besides anger, something like an endless desire to please other people, or a constant need to prove yourself, something that's got roots that go way, way deep, all the way down to an experience that's still holding you prisoner. Maybe you haven't fully processed an experience where there's someone it would help you to forgive (and maybe it's you). If that's the case—or if you're not sure whether it's the case, but your stomach is twisting up in knots, or your shoulders are getting tight and you suddenly feel funny even thinking about the issue of forgiveness as you're reading this—maybe talk to your sponsor about Step Four. And if you haven't got a sponsor yet, maybe get one.

Just saying. It's about survival.

61. A FIXED POINT OF NERDDOM

Melissa and I needed money, so I knew I was going to have to get a job.[57] I figured I would go back to auto parts, to what I knew. But I felt pretty sure that whatever job I got would end up boring the shit out of me (which, spoiler alert, it did).

One day, I was chatting with a buddy of mine, Davis—he'd been a friend and a customer at The Comic Outpost. Like me, Davis was bored with *his* day job. We came up with an idea that would help us beat the boredom. Before we pulled the trigger on the idea, though, I talked to my sponsor about what we had in mind.

Way back at the beginning of the book, I told you that obsessing over nerddom—some corner of pop culture that I loved without apologizing for it—was my first escape route from trauma, abuse and toxicity. Nerddom was a coping strategy for me back when I was a kid, and it remained a coping strategy for me while I was in the SLE. Of course, speed, cocaine and opiates had more recently been coping strategies—but the big distinction I need to draw here is that by the time I got to the SLE, I had figured out and knew in my bones that speed, cocaine and opiates were out to kill me. Nerd culture, on the other hand, wasn't.

> **Nerd culture:** The ideas, customs and social behaviors of people who are unashamed about expressing their opinions and enthusiasm about media content that matters to them on a personal level.

The loss of The Comic Outpost had left a big gap in my life. I'd loved talking to people about comic books and everything that connected to them. I told my sponsor that I needed to fill that gap with a project my buddy and I had cooked up, a project that connected to pop culture: to interacting with people about movies, comic books and TV shows I loved.

"That's fine," my sponsor said, "as long as sobriety comes first."

He didn't have to say any more. I got exactly what he was trying to get across, which was pretty simple: *If sobriety doesn't come first, you're screwed.*

That's the part I had lost sight of when I was running The Comic Outpost. I'd let the store, the experience of being the center of this exhilarating little world I'd created, come first. I'd let being the mayor of this little town I'd created become more important to me than my sobriety. I'd *chosen* to do that. And everyone who had any connection with me, large or small, everyone who counted on me in any way, ended up paying the price for that choice.

It sounds harsh when you say it, especially when you say it to someone who isn't in recovery, but if you're an addict, sobriety comes before your spouse.

Sobriety comes before your kids.

Sobriety comes before being a good son, a good daughter, a good friend.

If you fuck up on the sobriety front, you can't do anything but hurt any of those people. So you have to take care of yourself first.

Here's the flipside of that: Once you *do* make your own sobriety your priority, you can make being a good spouse, a good parent, a good son or daughter or a good friend *who you are*. You can make your service to those people who matter most to you, whoever they may be, your purpose in life. But not before.

So: as long as I didn't put the cart in front of the horse again (my sponsor was saying), I could be what I had loved being back when I owned a comic book store: the fixed point of nerddom. I could *exemplify* nerddom. I could have strong opinions about media content that mattered to me, and I could share those opinions without apology. I could tell the truth. My truth. As long as I put sobriety first.

On January 15, 2014, my buddy and I launched our podcast about nerd culture. It was just a hobby, something that would help me get my brain back. We didn't care if anyone listened to it. It was kind of like starting a punk band in someone's garage: we did it because we loved it. We did it because talking about the stuff we loved helped us to get through the day.

I called it *Nerdrotic*.

62. THE FINISH LINE THAT ISN'T

There is no finish line to sobriety, but there definitely is a finish line to cross once you start the marathon race of assembling a book like this. I'm about to cross that line. People are always telling me that I'm crossing lines that I'm not supposed to cross. Finally, I'm about to cross one I think everybody can agree needs crossing: wrapping up this book.

Recovery, for me, is a big jigsaw puzzle that extends outward in all directions forever with way too many missing pieces to count. You're always making connections and seeing where things fit together, but you never get the whole, definitive picture assembled once and for all. The picture just gets a little bit clearer every day...if you keep putting the pieces together.

It's been an honor and a pleasure sharing what I've been able to figure out so far about my personal recovery puzzle, which I'm lucky enough to still be working on, one day at a time. Before I share the final jigsaw piece that felt to me like it belonged in this book, I want to encourage you to share your story of dealing with addiction/alcoholism, either as an addict, as a loved one or family member of an addict or both.

You can always reach out to me at Gary@Nerdrotic.com. I try to read everything that comes in. I don't always read my mail as carefully as maybe I could (ADHD being what it is), and I don't always respond, but I do aim to read everything. Connecting with people means a lot to me. So please do reach out if reading my story has made you feel like you want to share yours.

Anyway, here's the end of my story.

***

It didn't take long for us to burn through the money we got from selling the shop. Melissa was working, but frankly, she was spread pretty thin. This was a two-income mortgage we'd taken on, and I had been AWOL financially for some time. Economically speaking, I was starting from scratch. I felt I had no choice but to stay in that auto parts job, but I knew that doing that job was not something that would make me feel happy or fulfilled.

Pretty much the only thing in my life that *was* making me feel happy and fulfilled, at least at first, was doing the *Nerdrotic* podcast. My buddy Davis had dropped out fairly early on, but I had kept going. I loved recording the episodes. I loved editing them. I loved uploading them. I loved hearing what people thought about them. In each of those podcasts, I got to express myself freely about the stuff that I loved. I got to call the latest developments in popular media *exactly* as I saw them. The honesty was exhilarating. When I felt some new movie or TV show really worked and was worth watching, I said so. By the same token, if something sucked, I got to be open and honest about that too.

Having that outlet made a real difference for me on a personal level. Sobriety became something I felt more and more comfortable sustaining, one day at a time—which is the only way to sustain it. My self-confidence, which had taken a hit after I sold the store, began to track upward again, back where it belonged. I started negotiating for, and getting, better job opportunities. I started earning more money. Honestly, having the podcast as a creative outlet was a big part of why all those things happened. Life had begun to make sense again for me.

Then this totally insane thing happened: the podcast really started to take off.

It was not unlike the way the store had taken off, but this time, the growth curve was a lot steeper. Over a period of four or five months, I'd built up a loyal and vocal audience. A lot of attention and effort went into those four or five months, a lot of care and commitment, a lot of taking care of the end-user's experience—but I'd done all of that because I knew that podcast was keeping me sane, and I knew I had to stay sane for the sake of my wife and kids.

But one day, I woke up and there was this side benefit to everything I'd been doing: the thing had blown up. In a good way, I mean. Listenership was through the roof.

By this time, in mid-2014, I was working at Tesla. I had a good job with good benefits, and Melissa and I were on our feet again financially. But I had this restless feeling. I knew the stuff I was doing in a Tesla warehouse was not what I was born to do. The stuff I was talking about on the podcast, on the other hand…

This wild idea came into my head. I sat down to talk about it with Melissa.

Despite all the damage I had inflicted and all the danger I had brought into her life, despite being forced into a position where she had to draw and defend some clear, non-negotiable boundaries for the sake of herself and her kids, Melissa had supported my recovery. She had bought me food and supplies when we both knew damn well that I couldn't be trusted with cash. She had welcomed my personal commitment to getting better and protecting myself—so I could get better and eventually be there again for my family.

She had kept a close eye on my progress, day by day and week by week. And once she'd gotten enough evidence that that progress was real, she had given me the benefit of the doubt again. She did that after I had burned her and lied to her and bullied her and left her working way too hard for way too long. She let me back into her life and into our house. She believed in me.

Which is not the same thing as saying she trusted me again—not yet. Not right away. I had to earn that. I had really done a number on the level of trust in our relationship, and I can't pretend here that I won all that trust back instantly, because I didn't. But Melissa did give me the chance to rebuild trust in our marriage, even though I had made some terrible choices and done almost everything a husband could do to destroy that trust. For giving me that chance, I will be grateful to her for as long as I live.

Whoever you are, wherever your journey in life happens to take you, whatever your mistakes and your failures may have been, my wish for you is that you have someone like Melissa in your life: someone who understands that the only real learning we can ever expect to put into practice is the learning that comes from examining where we fucked up as human beings. Someone who sees your potential. Someone who understands you well enough and compassionately enough to forgive what you were capable of in your worst moments.

Someone who knows what you're capable of in your best moments and wants you to have more of those.

Someone who, when you suggest something that other people would instantly dismiss—like quitting your job so you can focus full-time on building a YouTube channel—looks you in the eye, sees the person you were meant to be, believes in your ability to be that person and says the three words that make every good thing seem possible again:

"Go for it."

***

Most of the viewing audience for videos in general, and YouTube videos in particular, is people who are at work. People taking a coffee break, people watching (like I did at Tesla) when they think the boss won't notice, people with their headphones in while waiting in line at the bank or people doing chores around the house.

I believe that a sizable portion of those folks watching videos during their working day are people who feel just like I used to feel when I was at my lowest point, trying to make recovery work: lonely and wishing they weren't. They watch videos because the videos make them feel like they're not alone. I can't tell you how many people reach out to me to tell me that a video I made about a movie or TV show that mattered a lot to them helped them feel less alone while confronting a major challenge in their life: addiction, alcoholism, illness, the death of a loved one, you name it.

That's why I post videos about nerddom, and that's why I wrote this book: to let people know that they're not alone. Most of my life, I thought I was all alone. Eventually, I decided to open up to the idea that telling the truth and working on getting better as a person could bring the right people into my life—people I could support and people who would support me.

I hope what you've read here has given you the same kind of idea, particularly if you are in recovery or someone you love is in recovery. And I hope that, whatever it is you decide to love, you love every inch of it, and never apologize for loving it and finding out everything there is to find out about it.

One of my sponsors told me, "You know, Gary, if you're happy half the time, that's pretty fucking good." He was right.

It's a beautiful world. It's a dangerous world. Authenticity can heal trauma. And life is just too short for inauthenticity, including but not limited to dumpster-fire movies and television shows.

So: don't waste your time on bullshit. Find something else. Find something good. Find something that helps you learn more about who you are, something that makes you happy. Find someone who will celebrate you for exploring that thing and talking about that thing, honestly and without apology.

Then...go for it.

ACKNOWLEDGMENTS

To my ride or die, Melissa, whose encouragement and patience have proven more steadfast than the mightiest of Ents. Your encouragement has been precious.

To the merry band known affectionately as The Fellowship (and a very special thanks to Chris Gore for talking me into this), your camaraderie has served as a shield against the dark forces of doubt and a beacon of inspiration as we traverse the vast realms of the internet. Together, we have faced the trials of our quests, from the Shire to the farthest reaches of Mordor (or at least to the next coffee shop).

Remember always: You bow to no one!

ABOUT THE AUTHOR

Gary Buechler is a former comic shop overlord, current YouTube sensation and long-running podcaster known by his fans as Nerdrotic. Passionate about quality comics, movies and genre TV series created by POT (People of Talent), Buechler's broadcasts dissect the good, the bad and the ugly of current pop culture. Nerdrotic's frank opinions have delighted millions of geeks and gamers, made social justice warriors anxious and left bystanders wondering what just happened. *Waiting for Nerdrotic* is his first book.

ABOUT THE PUBLISHER

Legacy Launch Pad is a boutique publishing company that works with entrepreneurs from all over the world.

For more information about Legacy Launch Pad Publishing, go to: www.legacylaunchpadpub.com.

ENDNOTES

1 Alcoholism and drug addiction are family diseases.

2 Being abused by my teacher was another, of course.

3 He was an accountant by trade, and a damned good one. His clients—Dr. Seuss among them—loved him.

4 I didn't tell my parents about the abuse that had happened to me at school until I was maybe 19 years old. By then, my relationship with them was well and duly fucked up, and would stay fucked up for quite some time.

5 Dr. Strange: Master of the Mystic Arts had entered my life as an important presence by this point.

6 I would learn how wrong I was about that when I actually did land in prison, which turned out to be way different from high school—but I'll stop getting ahead of myself.

7 My alcohol and crystal meth addictions, as time went on.

8 I realize now that the quality of my work might not have been as great as I thought it was at the time, but hey, at least I had something to hand in.

9 But more on how I solved this problem later.

10 I never shot up, though, and I never touched opiates until much, much later…but we'll cover that particular trainwreck in another chapter.

11 From all I could tell, he never did.

12 "Can you fly this plane and land it?" "Surely you can't be serious!" "I am serious. And don't call me Shirley."

13 What you're about to read is one of the parts of this book where I need to be very clear that the choices I made were not good ones. I'm not proud of them, but I learned from them, and now I can look back on them and laugh. If somebody reading this finds humor in it, I'm fine with that, as long as they understand that the things I'm describing are not things I would ever want to do again or advocate for anybody else. My hope is that by honestly sharing some of my own stupid, laughable choices and their consequences, readers will be less likely to make equally stupid decisions and face equal or worse consequences—like, you know, dying. Please take everything I'm about to share in that spirit and don't be tempted to use drugs or alcohol like I did. It was not a smart lifestyle.

14 Not his real name, for the record. None of the names that show up in this book are real names except mine and Melissa's.

15 Though the crystal meth on the streets today is way stronger and even more addictive than what was available back then.

16 This was her asking me out. For the sake of full disclosure, I need to mention here that I never actually asked Melissa out on a date during this period. Pathetic.

17 This description either means a lot to you or nothing at all—it all depends on whether you were a teenager or a young adult in the late 1970s and early 1980s looking for new ways to make sense of a world that made no fucking sense.

18 Dr. Demento's show was another big pop-culture touchstone for me.

19 Who shall remain nameless…

20 An acronym for Community Resources And Self-Help.

21 Actually, this guy was a terrible choice for reasons that went far beyond him being the father of an ex-girlfriend. But I'm getting ahead of myself.

22 By the way, if there's one clear lesson you want to take away from this story, it might be that those little dogs are not a bad idea when it comes to home security.

23 Meaning prior convictions.

24 I had told Gerald all about CRASH.

25 Cigarettes are basically money on the inside.

26 His name was actually Cliff, I found out later.

27 Again, not a real name. Mostly because I don't want to give this guy any global publicity.

28 You've heard the expression "down in the hole"? Folsom is one of the places where you find out what that means.

29 For instance, he got a big kick out of asking me about my family, like he wanted to learn more about me and be best buddies. Then, he told me all the details of how he had killed those two kids my age before chowing down on their lunch.

30 Kyle was big on upper body strength. It was one of his obsessions.

31 It was what everyone was expecting.

32 "J-Cat" was what we called someone who was batshit crazy. Don't ask me why, it's just what we said.

33 Much later, during therapy, I would learn that when human beings are dealing with a traumatic situation in the present moment, it's typical for there to be moments of hyperfocused vigilance like this, moments that tune out everything but the threat that has to be overcome.

34 The Big Book gives alcoholics and addicts a comprehensive overview of the history of Alcoholics Anonymous (AA) as well as stories from people who have achieved and sustained sobriety through the program. It also offers resources and strategies to support alcoholics/addicts and their families. It's most famous for detailing the 12 Steps and 12 Traditions that serve as the foundations of AA. If you've made it this far through this book, it's a pretty good bet that you would benefit from reading the Big Book. The official title is *Alcoholics Anonymous: The Story of How Many Thousands of Men and Women Have Recovered from Alcoholism,*

35 I'm being ironic here, of course. Burying stuff only makes problems worse. If your personal history includes sustained trauma and/or childhood abuse, burying stuff is among the worst things you can do. The sooner you talk to a licensed therapist you click with, the better off you're going to be and the better off the people in your world are going to be.

36 I thought it would last forever, at the time, but of course it didn't. Sorry, I've fucked up the timeline—pretend you didn't see this. Just keep reading.

37 There had been a couple of women on the scene as I did my job in the procurement department at Folsom, but they had been motherly or auntie-like types.

38 By the way, this is a good place to point out to anyone starting the recovery journey that you really *do* need a team; this is not something you can do on your own.

39 At this point, they were sending me subtle signals that it was probably a good idea for me to go out and get a job of some kind, which I took to mean that they wanted

me out of the house as soon as possible. I found out later that they would have been happy for me to stay with them for as long as I needed to, but they believed, rightly, that it would be good for my recovery to work a regular job.

40 What I called "being freaked out" back then I now know to be complex post-traumatic stress disorder (C-PTSD). I should also point out that, years later, I did find a good therapist

41 I was filling up a *lot* of notebooks during this period.

42 It was called *Dark Legion*, by the way—today, you can consider it the ultimate collector's item.

43 I'm sure I can't say I'm super stable now either, but I do have a healthier lifestyle, for sure.

44 And a year after *that*, we were pregnant—but more on that later.

45 There are too many such people to list here, but Jamie Newbold of SoCal Comics and James Simm from Isotope Books were particularly helpful to me as I was finding my way as a comic store owner. This book wouldn't be complete without me saying how grateful I was, and am, for their help.

46 Little side note here: If you feel compelled to pull out a crayon at this point, you can color me libertarian.

47 There were a lot of ideas I came up with that *didn't* work, but they're nowhere near as much fun to talk about.

48 We could add a fourth nerd to this list: **Peter Jackson**, a confirmed Tolkien and Beatles nerd who has created wave after wave of content that does justice to the objects of his nerdhood.

49 Something else I call it: capitalism. No, that's not a dirty word.

50 If you're interested in finding out what the interior of The Comic Outpost looked like, just take a look at my studio as I'm doing one of my podcasts, videos or livestreams. It's the exact same vibe, with a few of the same pieces.

51 One of the things I worry about is whether this book paints a picture of Melissa as someone who never (or rarely) got exhausted, felt impatient or lost her composure. So, this is where I tell you that, as an addict, an entrepreneur and a guy with C-PTSD, I pissed my wife off in so many different dimensions and added ungodly stress to her life in so many different ways, that there were plenty of times she lost

her cool with me and said things she later regretted. Often enough, though, I had it coming.

52 Today, I still have that huge vinyl *Superman Returns* banner that I was trying to hang up in the store. I keep it in my house. I've got it hung up properly now, where I can see it every day. I like having that banner around as a reminder of how bad my decisions can be, how easy it is for me to go into autopilot mode when the stakes are way, way higher than I realize, how fucking stupid I am capable of being. How quickly the ladder can slip away. We now return to our regularly scheduled program.

53 It was around this time I decided, seemingly against all odds, to continue my less-than-stellar academic career. It was part of the whole connecting-with-people thing, being-on-stage thing. I wanted to amplify that. I got my high school equivalency certificate, and I took a 10-week editing course at San Francisco State in video production and media, picking up insights that helped me later on, when I decided to launch my YouTube channel. In retrospect, it was pivotal—I built a lot of my presentation and style myself over the years, but I owe a lot of the polish to SF State. To me, it's another reminder that it's never too late to teach an old dog some new tricks, just like it's never too late to start fresh. For anyone thinking of starting their own channel (I get emails all the time asking for advice), I would say that consistency is key—but so is investing in yourself (#neverstoplearning).

54 Note: The Melissa Method assumes that your family has two available vehicles. If your family doesn't have that, you'll need to find some way to get access to a vehicle you can use for a day or so that the addict/alcoholic can't use.

55 Melissa now was the only one with access to cash and bank accounts.

56 I was in the SLE for about six months. After the first 90 days there, I eased up a bit, but I always did at least one meeting a week, which is typically still my minimum. If I feel like I'm slipping, though, and that does happen, I will do two or three meetings *a day*.

57 Again: lots of people had day jobs at the SLE; you could come and go as you pleased, as long as you followed the house rules.